Lost & Found

Lost & Found

Joanna Wissinger

FOREWORD BY JULIE V. IOVINE

MACMILLAN PUBLISHING COMPANY
NEW YORK
MAXWELL MACMILLAN PUBLISHERS
NEW YORK   OXFORD   SINGAPORE   SYDNEY

A RUNNING HEADS BOOK

Macmillan Publishing Company
866 Third Avenue
New York, NY 10022

Macmillan Publishing Company is part of the Maxwell Communication Group of Companies.

Library of Congress Cataloging-in-Publication Data

Wissinger, Joanna.
Lost & found / Joanna Wissinger ; foreword by Julie V. Iovine.
p.   cm.
Includes bibliographical references and index.
ISBN 0-02-630590-9
1. Found objects (Art) in interior decoration.   I. Title.
II. Title: Lost and found.
NK2115.5.F68W5   1991
747′.9—dc20   91-11968
CIP

LOST & FOUND
was conceived and produced by
Running Heads Incorporated
55 West 21 Street
New York, NY 10010

Designer: Lesley Ehlers
Photo Editor: Ellie Watson
Photo Research: Tonia Smith and Linda Greer
Managing Editor: Lindsey Crittenden
Production Manager: Linda Winters

Special Sales Director
Macmillan Publishing Company
866 Third Avenue
New York, NY 10022

10 9 8 7 6 5 4 3 2 1

Typeset by Trufont Typographers
Color separations by Hong Kong Scanner Craft Company
Printed in Singapore by Tien Wah Press (Pte.) Ltd.

Acknowledgments

Thanks to everyone who worked on this book from the beginning, from editors Sarah Kirshner, who got me into it, through Charlie de Kay, who got me through it, to Mary Forsell, who finished the job. Ellie Watson did a terrific job finding beautiful photos.

Thanks to everyone who agreed to be interviewed and to kindly let me into their homes and studios, including Jon Bok, Robert Bellamy, Linus Corragio, Donald Lipski, Sally Prangley Rooney, Sam Milliken, Judyth van Amringe, Susan and Keith Kroeger, and Fro Vakili at BAM Construction/Design.

Much appreciation to Jim Elkind of Lost City Arts and Suzanne Lipschutz at Secondhand Rose.

Thanks to Sarah Stallard for her research in London.

Many thanks to Robin Cembalest for kindly reading the unfinished manuscript and providing many useful comments and emendations.

Last but not least, much gratitude and thanks to my husband, Paul Mann, for his patience, good humor, and willingness to share.

Contents

Foreword

Take a closer look around you. There's something happening to rooms that once were all white, stripped of distinguishing details, efficient "machines for living."

How many people do you know who have pillaged their local urban archeology store in search of decorative moldings to dress up the bare box of a new apartment? Maybe it's as subtle as standard-issue faucets replaced with old porcelain ones lettered in French. Or even a carved stone gargoyle that now spouts water in the bath, where before it was all shiny chrome. Shelves and mantels are decorated with the frog musicians and laughing skulls brought up from South American Day of the Dead celebrations. And the Salvation Army is no longer the exclusive domain of college dorm decorators—especially when those salvaged finds are transformed into elegant *objets* with a new coat of silver leaf. Such scenarios are a familiar sight these days. And yet, the tendency to reinvent, replace, and appropriate the old, the used, found objects, and art represents a profoundly new approach to home decoration.

This new sensibility is born of a wide-ranging confluence of ideas and concerns, among them: an environmental awareness of the need to recycle, a renewed arts and crafts movement where a show of the hand is prized over mass-produced standardization, a postmodern appreciation of the past, and an influx of cross-cultural influences. The art world, too, has offered up a mother-lode of inspiration for the home, from outsider art to collage—liberating our eye to see beyond the confining box of dogma. And, not to be underestimated, is an instinctive reaction against the bare-bones minimalism that was the sterile trademark of modernism and the prevailing norm of the post–World War fifties and sixties.

There's a spontaneous revolution afoot to bring color, texture, and personality into our lives and homes. We're redefining the word functional. A space no longer works just because it's easy to clean and there's an automatic button to operate everything from the stereo to the coffee maker. Today, rooms have to nourish our spirit as much as facilitate our daily routines.

Call it reincarnation of the everyday. If something's old, that doesn't mean it's trash. Found objects can have a second life, especially when taken out of context and seen with a fresh eye. But we're not decorating with junk. It's not enough to bring home an old plate. Try breaking it up into mosaics, burying it in a wall, or stacking it up into a vividly mismatched set. Make it fun, not precious. Wit and the visual doubletake are hallmarks of the new sensibility.

Above all, designing with found objects, salvaged goods, or naive art made from throwaway materials is about making connections with the past and toward the future. It's hard to beat the thrill of a flea market find. And recounting those sagas among friends introduces yet another dimension of pleasure in owning pieces that are somewhat less than pristine. It's a way not only to express personal style, but to savor it. Joanna Wissinger's *Lost & Found* opens the door onto a new world where the only limits are your own imagination.

Julie V. Iovine, March 1991

1

Decorative
Finds

Items that aren't "fine art" such as paintings, or expensive bric-a-brac such as silver bowls from Tiffany, generally fall under two headings: folk art and "found objects." Both categories can be difficult to define—but you know them when you see them. These elusive items are enjoying a renaissance with interior designers and others possessing strong personal style.

The anxieties of our high-tech age have inspired a renewed interest in tradition, in hand-wrought objects, in the efforts of the individual. The rapid rate of change in our society has created a phenomenon of instant "antiques": Even people in their twenties can be nostalgic for items from their childhood because they literally *don't* make them like that anymore. The landscape of childhood, those familiar objects that made up the setting of the past, has vanished from view. It's no wonder people are paying a lot of money for old Coke bottles.

But nostalgia is not the only impetus behind a love for odd, quirky, sometimes bizarre objects. There has been an explosion of interest in expressions of individuality, the unusual items that can't be bought in a store, that are not exactly what everybody else has. Perhaps it is a reaction to the conformity of the 1950s and early 1960s, the childhood of the baby boomers. Many grew up in the suburbs—oases of sameness and conformity —and secretly vowed that when they had their own homes, it wouldn't be that way. Certainly the history of this generation displays a desire for individuality and a rebellion against the expected.

Decorative objects, the kind you want to take home and cherish, can be found in many places besides museums and high-priced antiques shops. Once discovered, these items open up a range of imaginative possibilities in home design. Found objects can be displayed as sculpture, admired simply for their shape. Scavenged materials, found on building sites or in the trash, can be made into sculptures or useful objects. Folk art is most frequently simply displayed, but sometimes can be used for its original purpose (depending on the shape it's in).

Handmade and folk art items are often a clue to the hidden, secret life of the community. Because these objects bear the mark of the individual who made them, they seem to bridge the gap between ourselves and a world we don't and perhaps can never know. Although there are arguments on both sides for the superiority of the past over the present, it's perhaps the very distance and elusiveness that make it attractive.

Weathered folk art makes its greatest impact when displayed alongside contemporary objects. In this eclectic environment, opposite, various carved whirligigs and wooden life-size animals co-exist happily and harmoniously with contemporary art, classic modern furniture, and ethnic textiles. There's even latitude for whimsical touches, such as the ceramic "sweets" on the table in front of the sofa.

Folk Art

In recent years there has been an increased interest in the styles of the past, especially the furniture and decorative objects enjoyed by the wealthy. This interest in tradition extended toward the other end of the scale and the folk art boom was born.

Many pieces of folk art are quaint, amusing, historically interesting artifacts. Most folk art looks like anybody could do it. This is part of its charm. Indeed, most of the techniques involved are not technically difficult. The difficult part is unseen: the inspiration, the shedding of inhibitions that lets the creator go ahead and make some-

Quilts, often made of fabric scraps, are a wonderful way of recycling discarded and worn-out materials and turning them into art. Anyone with a talent for handiwork can create lively—and entirely original designs. This Freedom quilt, left, was made by Jesse Telfair of Georgia. A similar one is in the collection of the High Museum, Atlanta.

Even the most simply shaped utilitarian objects, such as this collection of ladles, right, can take on sculptural importance when massed and displayed.

thing. Many things now machine made used to be made by hand. Some of this is still available and much of it is beautiful.

Handmade elements are becoming more important and significant in contemporary art, design, and architecture. Nonelitist art made by "ordinary" people for their own use and pleasure has come into vogue. This art is independent of academic traditions. Its creators often lack formal training and are more interested in their own design than in the "correctness" of what they're doing. Much of what they make is simple in execution, although some pieces are quite complicated in the decoration.

Folk objects span the extremes of aesthetics, from raw to elegant. Folk artists create objects as a declaration of individuality, a personal need to create. Folk art may be utilitarian or it may be purely decorative but it always partakes of a personal and eccentric style. It can be found in the strangest places. Since, strictly speaking, it doesn't conform to most ideas of art, it has been made and then banished (by relatives, grandchildren, spouses) to storerooms, barns, trunks, jumble sales, flea markets, junk shops. Often, it survives only by chance, until spotted by an aficionado or collector.

Folk art objects, while most often highly individual, can be classified according to several broad categories. Ornament (often of found materials) endows them with personal and ceremonial character. Some impulses to adorn or create are artistic, others more practical, resulting in both decorative objects with function and purpose (to hold or support something) and embellished utilitarian forms. Some folk art objects served a practical purpose in their first existence, such as weather vanes and windmill weights. Others, such as hand-painted signs, were always intended to catch the eye and amuse or instruct.

Whatever their origin, they are an important reminder of the past and of individual experience. Depending on their nature, they can be incorporated into an interior in many ways: displayed as art or sculpture, hung on a wall, placed on a pedestal or in a case, tucked discreetly on a shelf to be discovered with delight. Would-be collectors can find them in various places: folk art galleries, junk shops, church sales, garage sales, in the attic, even in the trash, if you're lucky. Part of their charm comes from the fact you can't buy them in department stores. But keep your eyes open, check out the most likely sources (particularly in rural areas, remote from big-city ways), and you're sure to turn up a treasure or two.

Weather Vanes & Whirligigs

These are very popular folk art objects to collect and display. Weather vanes, washed with the patina of age, have iconic associations with rural living. Yet they work well as art objects because they were originally designed as decorative, three-dimensional presences. Their outlines are recognizable but not detailed, adding to their sculptural simplicity. There is often wit in their exaggeration of scale.

The animal figures on this poolside patio, below, are a motley assortment, lovingly assembled over time by a dedicated collector. Selecting a theme is the first and hardest step—whether it is a favorite beast, a flock of varied birds, a mixture of safari animals, or an entire menagerie. After that, collecting a favorite object is usually an easy task, especially if you regularly visit flea markets, junk shops, and other sources of lost and found items.

The rural motifs of whirligigs and weather vanes harmonize with even the most sophisticated environments. Whirligigs use wind power to make a carved figure perform an action, such as the man sawing wood above. The stronger the breeze, the faster he saws. Weather vanes often incorporate farm animal images—such as cows, horses, and the familiar rooster. Even when in repose, these rustic items are interesting artifacts.

Many common weather vane motifs are inherently symbolic, such as roosters (strength), eagles (nobility), and doves (peace). Horses are another important category: racing horses, horse and rider, horse and buggy, jumping horse. A Native American kneeling to draw his bow is also a recurring image, as is an angel with a trumpet—Gabriel blowing the trumpet on Judgment Day? Farm implements and animals—accompaniments of daily life—are also popular. Even emblems of urban life, such as the inventions of the machine age, appear as weather vanes: trolley cars, locomotives, automobiles.

Weather vanes were constructed of various materials. Some, made of copper hammered into molds and then gilded, were produced in factories. These could be ordered by mail. Others were made by skilled individuals—farmers, woodworkers, blacksmiths, tinsmiths. Some were ornamented with cut-out motifs, including hearts and stars. Materials such as wood or tin didn't last as long as copper, so examples are rarer.

Whirligigs, another type of wind-powered folk art object, have elements meant to spin around in moving air; their speed shows the strength of the breeze (or gale, as the case may be), in contrast to weather vanes, which indicate the direction of the wind. Whirligig figures often perform a task, such as sawing wood, rowing a boat, or riding a bicycle. Others display animals in motion—including horses, dogs, cats, roosters, cows, birds—flying or running, for example.

Decoys

Decoys—sculpted, carved replicas of ducks and other game birds—are considered the only truly American folk art. Used by professional hunters (market gunning was a recognized profession until it was banned in 1913), they were often made by the same people. Now, hunting is a popular seasonal sport. Stylistically, decoys fall into one of two categories: They are either perfect replicas of a particular bird species or a stylized interpretation. It doesn't matter to a duck (they have poor eyesight), but most hunters and carvers are firmly on one side or the other. Some examples are the sculptural essence of duck, sandpiper, Canada goose, or swan. Others can't be told from the real thing. Another type of decoy was used for fish spearing, particularly large species like garfish and sturgeon. These take the form of life-size replicas (on the theory, one supposes, that the sight of an apparently undisturbed compatriot would lure skittish fish within stabbing range).

Canes

Embellished with carvings of heads, decorative tracery, or animal figures, canes are highly personal objects. Some of the best examples come from the American South, where walking sticks, as they are known, are a cultural tradition. Cane carving is a whittler's art, the province, often, of elderly men in rural areas. The end result often derives from initial shapes seen in branches and roots. Because canes are held in the hand, they are among the most intimate of objects.

Signs

Hand-painted signs often manifest a charm of their own, a kind of "folk graphics" in contrast with the usual slickness displayed by professional graphic artists. Invigorated by their freedom from conventional restraints, amateur sign painters tend to indulge their imaginations with decorative and ornamental letterforms. This interpretation of the alphabet, still recognizable despite liberties taken, has an air of playfulness and spirited interpretation, full of invention and enthusiasm. These "naive" signs can be lots of fun to have around—reassuring proof of their maker's confidence in the power of words. And signs need not have recognizable folk art origins. Contemporary, high-tech signs can make an effective statement, too—often as iconography as well as decoration.

Shop signs in the form of oversized objects date back to an era when much of the populace was unable to read. Lettered signs were supplemented with eye-catching depictions of trademark wares or symbolic forms. These signs can be classified as "graphic equivalents"—symbols that represent goods or services. Some of them, highly abstracted, are still with us—the barber's pole, the pawnbroker's triple balls—as fast-disappearing remnants of a simpler age.

Some signs displayed considerable ingenuity on the part of the maker. Shoemakers displayed giant shoes and boots in various states of repair. It's traditional for fish-

An assortment of unlikely objects brings a certain vitality and energy to a Manhattan loft, right. Chief among the assemblage are a collection of commemorative china plates and two large neon beer signs.

monger's shops to display carved or painted fish. One bait-shop sign, dating from about 1930–40, was marked by an innovative use of materials: a fish was incised on a wood rectangle, the shiny silver scales made from beer-can tabs.

These signs have an amusing quality and are often quite appealing. Because they were designed to be immediately recognizable, such signs possess a strong sculptural and graphic nature that increases their decorative usefulness. They also have a pop-art quality of being larger or smaller than life. Not all signs that make effective objects have a folk art origin. Contemporary or product signs can make an effective statement, too. Like the much more sophisticated and knowing work of sculptor Claes Oldenberg, these naive sculptures prove that ordinary objects possess unexpected interest and beauty.

Cigar-Store Indians

Native Americans, identified in the popular imagination as the first to cultivate tobacco, quickly became the nineteenth-century symbol of commerce in cigars and pipe tobacco. Cigar-store Indians are still a well-known and beloved symbol in the minds of many, but have otherwise disappeared from sight (when was the last time you saw one?).

Nineteenth-century examples range from crude to sophisticated. Most figures were wooden, ornately carved and painted. Later ones were made of cast and painted metal. Some have elaborate drapery, that is realistically painted. Others were mere stick figures with bottle caps for eyes and braids made of twisted rope. Some were adorned with wigs of human hair, dangling metal earrings inserted in carved lobes, and quivers filled with carved arrows. Some hold tobacco leaves or cigars in raised hand, as though offering passers-by a smoke. Not all cigar-store Indians were braves or chieftains. Some were maidens with long braids and sweet expressions.

Ceramics

Clay is a malleable material, allowing a wide range of styles and approaches. Some of the more interesting finds around are pottery vessels decorated with human heads, usually African-American heads or faces, made after hours by factory workers in the Midwest and South during the second half of the nineteenth century. These are known variously as slave jugs, face vessels, voodoo pots, grotesque jugs, plantation pottery, or effigy jugs. Fashioned with varying levels of skill, they are often delightfully frivolous. Other common ceramic objects—most part of standard factory production—include figurines, decorated jugs, and flasks. These might be adorned with flowers, costumed literary characters, and abstract ornament, ranging from simple to intricate in style.

Another interesting form of ceramic decoration can sometimes be found in secondhand shops or flea markets and is becoming increasingly popular (couturier Christian Lacroix, known as an arbiter of cutting-edge taste, even has a few examples in his Paris apartment). Often called "Debrism," "Bits and Pieces," or *pique assiette* (French for "stolen pieces"), this popular turn-of-the-century hobby craft involved covering a jar or vase (sometimes even a small piece of furniture) with wet cement, then covering it with small objects and memorabilia, bits and pieces of broken ceramics, tile, and small shells, for example, and letting the cement dry. Some objects, particularly mirrors and picture frames, were then covered over with metallic gold or silver paint. Others were left plain.

Carnival & Entertainment Objects

Carnivals and amusement arcades are another rich source of found decorative objects, which were designed to catch the eye, amuse, entice, and induce an audience to spend money. Among the possibilities are shooting-gallery targets, ring-toss figures and ball-toss targets, painted and carved figures used in carnival minstrel shows, handmade puppets and ventriloquists' dummies, and fun-house figures. Your appreciation for these objects may well depend on the strength of your taste for the outrageous.

Carousel and merry-go-round sculpture associated with childhood pleasures have an uncomplicated appeal. They are cartoonish, decorated, brightly colored, and often superbly carved. Ornament includes carved and painted sprays of flowers and embossed and "jeweled" decorative harnesses, further elaborated with touches of gilt.

A paper headdress, right, is an amusing interpretation of Native American ceremonial regalia. Boldly promoting Washington State apples by surrounding its lettering with a corona of "feathers," this piece of advertising art is even more striking surrounded by apple-related images.

Carousel figures aren't limited to horses and ponies. Other animals (some much larger than life) include peacocks, reindeer, sea horses, tigers, giraffes, rabbits, and lions. Another site for applied fantastic ornament was the side panels on carousel wagons (intended for the use of the timid or elderly). These wagons were often drawn by teams of fabulous beasts—camels, cats, panthers—exotic creatures wearing fanciful harnesses. More familiar animals, such as pigs, were sometimes also found.

The circus was also the locus of intriguing objects and carved fantastic imagery, found as part of rides, wagons, posters, and games.

Chalkware

Chalkware, made of molded and painted plaster, was a less expensive alternative to the ceramicware that was popular in the latter half of the nineteenth century. Common figures are animals, birds, and angels. Many chalkware pieces have sentimental themes, such as a rabbit with a nodding head or a small child clutching a dove. Each figure was colorfully and individually painted. Since plaster is a fragile material, few antique examples of chalkware have survived, but much is available in reproduction today.

Religious objects—such as this carved and painted figure, above—are prized by many collectors for their craftmanship. This one is displayed with dramatic candles in a churchlike setting. For other collectors, such as Los Angeles–based sculptor and furniture maker Jon Bok, religious designs have a populist energy. In an interior designed by Bok, right, an altar-style chair is decorated with bottle caps. Though the hubcaps on the wall have no religious significance, they seem to have a ceremonial purpose.

Disparate elements come together to create a powerful still life, below. A hand-carved and -painted standing crucifix is displayed with a pub sign and an unconventional chair with a wood sculpture resembling a watermelon.

Religious and Symbolic Objects

Images with mystical, religious, or spiritual connotations are another intriguing subdivision of decorative objects. These include carved or painted statues, figures, and reliefs depicting snakes, devils, angels, Adam and Eve, the Garden of Eden, Christ with sheep, and the Crucifixion scene. Other popular symbolic figures are the Statue of Liberty, Uncle Sam, skeletons, Egyptian figures, and hearts, to name but a few.

Figures of saints and angels are often collected and displayed in niches as sculpture. Many inhabitants of the art, fashion, and entertainment worlds delight in the powerful, naive, and intriguing imagery and symbolism (stars, crescents, crosses) of these figures. Orthodox Greek and Russian icons, small painted images of saints distinguished by a flattened, naive style of portraiture, are another variation that has strong appeal, enhanced by the glitter of gold. Nineteenth- and early–twentieth-century Christian objects are part of the trend, which began with interest in third-world religious items, such as voodoo and santería figures from the Caribbean and Latin America.

Southwestern Santos are another type of religious figure, prized for their powerful mysticism. These strong images demonstrate a strong Mexican-Catholic influence, reminiscent of Day of the Dead celebratory objects: skulls and skeletons adorned with brightly painted garlands of flowers.

Gravestones and other cemetery and funereal objects can sometimes be found for sale. These generally display images of angels, and other, more overtly religious symbols, such as crosses or Stars of David. Others bear chiseled, evocative terms such as MEMORY or PEACE. These are poignant in their emotional power and impressive in terms of the weight and palpability of the materials, often stone or marble.

Fine Native American objects and found furniture lend mellow energy to these interiors, above and opposite. Natural materials—in one case, a massive chimney made of rough native rock, in the other, rich panelled walls—provide a complementary background to the collected objects on display. The effect is not that of a "decorated" room, but one created naturally over time.

Portraiture, Faces, and Figures

The human figure is a popular motif in folk art. It appears on a wide variety of objects, including carved busts, molded ceramic jugs, ships' figureheads, and items used as in-store advertising displays for patent nostrums. Advertising art is a rich trove that includes such items as figures made of brushes, haberdashery wooden forms for displaying hats, and naively painted mannequin heads. Apothecary display forms, faces with amusing protruding tongues, were used to promote pills at the turn of the century. Phrenology heads, diagrammed with arcane lines and charts, were used to teach phrenology, a Victorian pseudoscience that claimed to be able to determine personal characteristics from skull bumps and shape of head (a nineteenth-century version of the Minnesota Multiphasic Personality test).

Antique wooden mannequins can often be found in secondhand and antiques shops. Displayed in groups of two, three, or more on a table, these have a sensuous, sculptural presence, evoking classical statuary. Handmade dolls are another delightful find. Articulated figures are a step beyond busts and static images, carved or cast in one piece. These have arms and legs that move. Often they bend at the waist, elbow, wrist, and the knee as well. A limberjack is a figure with flexible stick or wire attached to its lower back and then to a handle. With a bit of skill, it can be jiggled and joggled into performing all kinds of acrobatics.

Home hardware, such as towel holders, coat hooks, and so on, occasionally turns up in the form of hands and arms. Fraternal orders often used anthropomorphic ballot boxes in the shape of a man's head or skull. Handmade protective gear for workers at bygone factories sometimes appears for sale. It is so remote from modern protective gear that it has the archeological air of armor or primitive tribal masks.

Animal Figures

Animal motifs rival the human face and figure as a popular subject. Some examples memorialize a particular animal, perhaps a beloved pet. Others are just for fun, or represent a symbolic animal, such as a lion or an eagle, diminutive and tamed. Rocking horses, a sculptural toy, display a wide range of diversity and stylization. Animals also appear as architectural ornament. Some fulfilled a practical purpose, such as the carved snakes that were used in barns to scare off rats and mice.

Scrimshaw animals, carved from whalebone, occupied sailors' leisure hours. Animal figures often show a sense of humor as well as art. Dogs are especially adorable and turtles are also popular. But almost every species of animal—from peacocks to hippos and giraffes—shows up, fabricated from an equally diverse range of materials, including (but certainly not limited to) furniture parts and bottle caps.

Fish have an innate appeal. Some versions are realistically detailed with gills and scales; others are flat and cartoonlike. They appear in a number of different functions: used by fishermen as lures or decoys, topping weather vanes, serving as signs or doorstops. Scales can be made of various materials. Almost anything will do: bottle caps, bits of mica, mirror, glass, pull-tabs from beverage cans (now all but unknown). If not be-scaled, they are often painted in various ways. Some have working (or at least movable) fins.

Birds are also popularly and extensively represented. The eagle, with its powerful iconographic presence, is a common American subject. Folk art birds are portrayed in various materials using a variety of techniques such as painting, chip carving (see page 34), and applied ornament. Birdhouses and birdcages have their own presence, often becoming elaborately ornamented miniarchitecture.

Wild animals do not go unrepresented. Domesticated, appealing figures of deer, moose, squirrels, turtles, and snakes (some of them jointed) abound. They are carved, painted, and etched for decoration.

Decoration with Found Objects

The patina of use is a trend now in stylish interiors. While in the past, rust, grime, and tarnish were banished at the first smear, they are now positively welcomed. Rusty metal chandeliers, rough-hewn chairs wrought by blacksmiths, tables made of recycled lumber—all such items appear in the best homes. By the same token, matching colors and patterns are not nearly as important as they used to be. Historic periods and styles don't have to match. Common rocks, tin washbowls, and old china are just as significant as silver candlesticks and porcelain bowls of potpourri. This look is about mixing beautiful fragments: antique chandelier crystals, perhaps, displayed against a carved stone block found in a church, for a look that's spare yet romantic. It's also about contrast—a table with a lacy, curlicued metal base topped with a weathered slab of old marble.

How to achieve this mix of antique and not-so-antique? While some go to great lengths in re-creating a timeworn interior, others are more casual. The general effect is of interesting times out on show. "Pieces get added and the ones you get bored with go," says one aficionado of this manner of decoration. Perhaps it's that simple.

The unexpected encounter of a silver songbird—which might have once perched on a trophy or been a hood ornament—with weather-beaten cherubs results in a one-of-a-kind *objet*, right.

**Artistic
Finds**

Artists in Spite of Art

Out on the mysterious periphery of traditional folk art lies an unconventional band of artists who, ignoring the orthodox way of doing things, make art, furniture, or architecture out of whatever materials are on hand, recycling discards and incorporating junk. The resulting objects exert a strange fascination on many viewers. This type of art is known by many names and it comes from unexpected sources. Its creators are often uninhibited by education or training (or their lack thereof). They are most often elderly or retired people, who seem filled with a desire to express all the things they have not been able to during a lifetime of hard work.

This type of art lacks a precise definition. It is sometimes referred to as primitive or naive art, and this term may well convey some sense of the attitude of its creators. Their art appeals because it is so open. It's clear that they have not learned but instead understood, instinctively, how to make art. Everything about the piece and its maker is shared with the observer—technique, materials, construction. Outsider art, as it is often called, is not trendy in its intention. It teems, rather, with unexpected visual forms. Much of it, in fact, is anonymous.

But many academically trained artists seek to acquire these characteristics: directness, crudity, childlike clarity, and candor. Despite its lack of polish, outsider art has a dedicated body of admirers. Its popularity has grown in recent years, as more and more dealers have become interested in buying and selling examples.

What is outsider art? This category can consist of many different examples, all coming from widely different origins. It might be an intriguing group of figures made of tightly twisted wire, wound with scraps of paper and ribbons, found on the sidewalk in front of a transient hotel in Philadelphia, their maker unknown. Yet, some outsider artists *are* known. Georgia-born Bessie Harvey makes dolls from wood and cloth, human and animal hair, feathers and broken jewelry, inspired by figures she claims to see in visions. Tennessean Hawkins Bolden, blinded at an early age, occupies himself making masks out of a variety of found materials (aluminum pans, scraps of wood, and fabric) as a form of protection against mysterious forces. The late Thomas Trapani made furniture and shrinelike objects from found materials, including feathers, wood, and paint.

Just as Bessie Harvey is inspired by visions and Hawkins Bolden makes protective masks, much outsider art has a strong mystical and religious, often obsessive, content. Another well-known outsider artist is the Reverend Howard Finster, who believes he can reach people through his art as well as through preaching. His religious beliefs are a strong influence on his art, which often contains painted Bible quotes and figures of angels. The late James Hampton, also a preacher, is remembered for his work *Throne of the Third Heaven*, now in the Smithsonian's National Museum of American Art. The work, constructed over a long period of time in an unheated garage "studio" in downtown Washington, D.C., consists of a series of altars, made of junk and trash—old furniture, insulation board, cardboard tubes, burnt-out bulbs—all carefully covered with gold and silver foil.

When decorating rules break down, what often emerges is a collection in which unusual elements work together. Opposite, those elements include an étagère, painted by Keith Haring in his distinctive style, as well as a painted art deco screen and a tall, neo-pop sculpture made of colorful fabrics and other soft materials.

Artists' Spaces

Another characteristic of this type of art is its tendency to take over an entire room or house—or even to *be* a house. There are many environment makers. As with creators of specific objects, some are famous, others are not. In Brooklyn, New York, for example, eighty-three-year-old Joseph Furey spent five years covering the walls and ceilings of his apartment with abstract patterns made up of over seventy thousand objects, including painted cardboard bow ties, cut-out hearts, real clamshells, plaster chickens, scraps of wallpaper, pieces of mirror, and bits of tile—the whole thing covered with varnish and dabbed with paint. His efforts were not discovered until he moved out to live with his son's family.

A similar work was created by the man known as "Creek Charlie," whose real name was Charlie Fields. He was the youngest of several children in a small town in Mississippi. After the rest left home, he lived with his mother for several years until she passed away. After her death, he slowly began to transform the house. He painted the house inside and out with stripes, squiggles, and polka dots, enclosing the porch with a lattice of soda-pop bottles and hanging model airplanes from the ceiling. At one time, the exterior of the constantly changing house was wired with tiny blinking Christmas lights. During his lifetime, Charlie Fields had an open house every Sunday, when many of the residents of the nearby countryside came to visit and play.

Perhaps the most famous example of this type of environment is Simon Rodia's Watts Towers in eastern Los Angeles. Rodia, an Italian immigrant, created these strange structures in the 1950s, using a wire armature encrusted with broken china and other bits pressed into mosaic patterns. Little is known about why he created these idiosyncratic towers, using only humble found materials.

Tressa "Grandma" Prisbrey, another eccentric Californian, was the builder of Bottle Village, an environment consisting of a group of tiny houses, constructed of materials

Joseph Furey lived in an apartment in Brooklyn, New York, for many years, but it was not until after his wife's death that he began his obsessive decoration of the walls—ultimately covering every inch with various shapes cut out of thick cardboard and daubed with bright paint, left and right. The hearts are a tribute to his late wife. While not every homeowner may have the dedication to cover entire walls with such painstaking detail, Furey's work is testimony to the imaginative and entirely personal style that comes from individual ideas. Such is the power of looking to one's own experience for inspiration, rather than following prescribed design examples.

One-of-a-kind tramp-art objects show off the characteristic motifs of the genre— zigzag, diamond, and star shapes made up of chip-carved layers of scrap wood, right. The dizzying geometric display exerts a strong fascination. Picture frames and wall-hung letter holders, as well as small boxes, are typical finds.

from the city dump. Entire child-size buildings were made of such castoffs as old soda bottles, pencils, and abandoned doll's heads, decorated with buttons and pull-tabs from beer cans. The walkways between the diminutive structures were paved with old license plates, commercial signs, scissors, and other debris.

Tramp Art

Tramp art is a fascinating subdivision of outsider art. It was made during the 1860s to the 1930s, mainly by itinerant wanderers of Middle European heritage, who had learned the technique as a traditional craft. In the New World, they incorporated industrial materials, such as cigar-box and fruit-crate wood. The final result was the transformation of an established folk craft into something rich and strange. Examples of tramp art we see today seem to be little messages from the past, anonymous gifts of a ghostly band of whom not much is known.

The technique involved, which requires little skill and can be done without special tools, is known as chip carving. It consists of gouging regular chips from a surface and

Tramp-art frames hold pride of place on a bedside table, right. A Mission lamp and pique assiette pencil holder contribute to the eclectic selection. A colorful, framed display of artists' penholders, hung on the wall above the table, is another touch.

using these incisions to build up a regular geometric or abstract pattern, using thin pieces of scrap wood. Often, sheets of wood are layered to create the effect of raised ornament. Some applied and inlaid decoration is also found. One example of a tramp-art frame is covered with actual kitchen implements (knife, fork, spoon, bone from lamb chop, spools of thread), which were then painted gold. A few examples are carved with dates and simple motifs such as hearts.

Most tramp-art pieces were copied from machine-made objects and then themselves served as models for other pieces by tramps. Examples of different types of items include picture frames, boxes, comb cases with bits of mirror for a last sprucing up before going out, and pincushions. Many small chests of drawers incorporate secret compartments. Decoration includes decals, paint, beads, upholstery tacks arranged in patterns, and bits and pieces of china and colored stone.

The peculiar charm of tramp art (and it's not for everyone) lies in its excessive decoration—sometimes to the point of what many would call ugliness. Tramp-art pieces have a fascination because they incorporate a rich hodgepodge of ornamental designs, lavished on objects that are really quite humble. The magic of tramp art lies in its simple, incised decorations, which, repeated to an extreme degree, become complex and ornate.

Sculpture from Junk

It's not difficult to incorporate this type of art into your own life. Sources of inspiration abound, from traditional found objects known to primitive man, such as feathers, bones, shells, and pebbles, to artifacts of the modern age, including cans, bottles, rope, string, and plastic. The world is full of trash that can be used again. In fact, there is probably more discarded stuff now—more reusable things that go to waste—than ever before. Available materials are at an all-time high. Discards and *objets trouvés* (a French term meaning "found objects") are a significant element in the mainstream of twentieth-century art. The contemporary spirit of recycling and care for the environment extends to art as well.

But how to pick out the items you need from a world overflowing with trash? Slow down and look. Develop your eye. Try to cultivate a sensitivity to elements and textures. When you're just starting out, relax and experiment. It's important to realize that the artistic merit has nothing to do with price, elegance, prestige, prettiness, or even cleanliness. Often, qualities generally deemed unattractive, such as rust, corrosion, or peeling paint, actually possess great beauty, lending visual variety and richness to a piece.

What sort of materials are you looking for? Anything that you want to work with. Materials might include burlap, mirrors, charred wood, rusted metals, plastics, machine parts, even magazine clippings. Artists have made sculpture and assemblages using everything from washing machine agitators to car grilles, windshield wipers, heavy pulleys, and metal boxes. Common "found" materials that are effective and easy to work with include lumber, house paint, car paint, wax crayons, aluminum foil, and broken crockery.

A great deal of work must have gone into a wreath of barbed wire, entwined with domestic fragments such as a rusted fan blade and the remains of a coffee pot, right. It has its softer side as well, as shown by further decorative touches including colorful autumn leaves and small glass bottles holding blooms.

A discarded heater gets a second life through the decorative use of buttons and beads, above left. The art of "bits and pieces"—also known as pique assiette—uses ceramic fragments, pressed into putty, to ornament and embellish the surface of an existing vessel, such as this urn by Rebecca Cross, above right. Ordinary household objects—plates, mugs—can be covered with broken crockery to create this look, often displayed on surfaces like walls and lampposts.

Where to look? Drawers, cupboards, gutters, attics, basements, backyards, alleys, and dumps. Natural objects might turn up almost anywhere. Your chances of discovering a thing of pure abstract beauty in the trash are high. The next step is to enhance its existing qualities. Concentrate on the texture and rhythm of objects in your assemblage. If you have several items that are the same or similar, experiment with the beauty of repetition.

Found objects can be arranged in several ways. They can be restrung as mobiles, suspended singly as sculptural pieces, or used as an applied ornament on a flat surface. If you have many shards and bits and pieces of wood, ceramic, or glass, you can create a mosaic texture on any flat surface.

Sculptural assemblages could include rusted gears, bits of rope, weathered clamps, and farm machinery parts. Another might incorporate old saw blades, bicycle chains, metal washers, bolts, paint scrapers, hinges, a fan pump, a flashlight holder, and an electric switch and light socket. Your assemblage need not be complex or incorporate more than a few types of objects. Early in his career, Greek-American artist Lucas Samaras made several small sculptures consisting of glass vases filled with bits and pieces of broken glass, mirror shards, and china, carefully cleaned and sorted. They are quite serene and beautiful.

Some found objects—such as beach pebbles, abalone shells, scraps of discarded metal, and bits of weathered wood—have an intrinsic beauty that makes them suitable for use as jewelry. Anything small can be holed and strung on fine wire, chain, or string to make bracelets or necklaces. It's easy to make earrings with inexpensive jewelry findings.

Don't leave your children out. Kids are naturals at transforming junk into art. Just make sure that they work with safe objects with no dangerous sharp edges.

Functional
Finds

A "found" mosaic is made of cracked and broken tile, carefully fitted together and then placed atop a large terra cotta flowerpot to create a charmingly impromptu fountain, below. A similar approach marks this spiral stair, opposite, where random tiles, from unglazed gray to flowered bathroom tile, adorn each step.

What makes a find "functional"? Each object considered here has a purpose. Each is a response to immediate circumstances: I need a place to sit down, to do my laundry, to eat my lunch. Beyond the immediate, tangible need lies a spiritual need: I want something beautiful. The makers (sometimes re-makers) of these objects work from an aesthetic that combines a desire for beauty with a response to the needs and resources of the immediate environment. Materials don't have to be brought from some exotic, expensive place—an Italian quarry or a Brazilian rainforest. Instead, they originate in the here and now—artistically combining the materials at hand: anything from bone, shell, and hair to wood, car parts, beer cans, and cardboard boxes. This ad hoc process results in personalized and witty objects. Their inventiveness creates a curious attraction in the mind and heart of the viewer.

Why do we want these battered, beat-up, handmade objects when we could have new, shiny ones, straight from the showroom or factory? Perhaps because these objects stimulate our natural interest and sense of self. In our industrial, high-tech society, machines make everything for us. Inventive handmade furniture and objects represent a break from this standardization, a memorial to the significance of individuals. The recycling of waste into beauty is another aspect of their appeal. Part of their charm comes from their reinvented context, familiar objects presented anew in different surroundings. We are reminded of the original power of the cliché that led to its use in the first place.

For example, a pineapple-shaped finial, in its original place on a building, is simply part of that building and of the overall decorative scheme. But removed and displayed on a pedestal, it is a piece of sculpture, a beautiful thing in and of itself, as well as a reminder of the care and importance once lavished on architectural details. Taken out of its context the door of a 1940 Ford automobile, or the bumper of a Packard, when hung

on the wall, also beguiles the eye. Recycled and reused, these objects make us understand that the world around us is made up of many beautiful and meaningful parts.

Irony and nostalgia play a part as well. Irony because that sculpture on the wall that delights the eye and draws approving comments is really just a car door. Nostalgia because it's a kind of car that isn't made anymore and hasn't been for a long time and maybe your father or grandfather had a car like that.

What kind of things can play these reborn roles in our lives, getting a second chance on stage? Furniture is certainly a major factor in this category, as are fabrics and wallpapers. Not only does furniture last for generations, it can also be created anew from recycled parts. Fabrics and wallpapers, sometimes preserved for years in the time capsule of a warehouse or storeroom, are a breath of air from the past, bringing back rooms still extant only in memory. Humbler items, such as washing machines, stoves, and refrigerators participate in this renaissance, too.

Flea Market Finds

One fairly simple way of bringing found furniture—furniture with history—into your life is to buy it. It's easy to find. Flea markets, swap meets, and antiques fairs can be a useful source for good secondhand furniture. Sometimes you can find perfectly decent furniture on the street (a time-honored urban method of apartment furnishing), at unprepossessing junk shops, or even in the garbage. Furniture has a way of lasting forever, especially if it was made well in the first place. Many a living room is furnished with someone's grandmother's or great-aunt's parlor set.

For some, seeking out furniture in good condition to use it again is only the beginning. They enjoy refinishing old furniture to look like it did when new. Others go a step further, completely making it over (sometimes unrecognizably so) with a new paint job, new upholstery, and new hardware.

A few ideas of what you can do to a piece of furniture: Paint it. Refinish it. Re-cover it. Change hardware. Add mirror, shelves, or applied ornament. Stencil it. Put wheels on it. Paint it with a faux finish, such as marble, tortoiseshell, or malachite. Leave it as it is.

Old screens can be refinished and covered with fabric. Tables can be painted or given a faux finish. Chairs with wooden frames might get faux finishes or a simple coat of paint in an exciting color; upholstered pieces get fresh, new upholstery or an intriguing (transparent, beaded, bowed, or ruffled) slipcover. Old steamer trunks can be cleaned and used as tables, cushioned for seating, or simply displayed (very useful for hidden storage) for decorative purpose in a room.

Born-Again Furniture

While to many the word "furniture" implies foursquare wooden tables and staid upholstered wing chairs, to others it opens up a whole world of adventurous possibilities.

Functional does not mean unadorned. The judicious application of various colors of paint has turned these old dining chairs, opposite, into decorative objects in their own right.

There are designers, architects, and artisans who revel in making new furniture out of the most unlikely bits and pieces of things: hay bales, flower pots, industrial scraps, fire hose nozzles.

Strategies for found furniture, furniture made art, are simple: the reuse of existing resources. Sometimes the great discovery comes when you find out how one object—such as a plastic food bin—can be made to do double duty as a drawer. These "multiple-function objects" are a source of inspiration and delight. You can enjoy their wit as you appreciate their usefulness.

The pleasures of born-again furniture stem as much from the mind as the eye. The use of recycled elements is both amusing and thought provoking. Designers, whether known artists or anonymous craftspeople, seem to share a similar aesthetic: No matter how carefully such pieces are made, they can't get rid of a nonchalant air, as though they have been simply slapped together. Yet they show an appreciation of function, often carefully worked out. The use of recognizable elements, such as a gear-shift knob for a handle or a bottle cap as an ornament, creates connections between this object and the whole class of things using the same detail, bringing a simple chair or table into a relationship with a wider world. Nostalgia plays a part in these associations as well. Old things are recognized. Old associations are brought to mind anew, or perhaps contradicted by new use.

Part of the charm of reborn furniture comes from the suspicion that you—had you the time, the inspiration, and the tools—could have made the chair or table in question yourself. It has the appeal of the underdog—humble materials transformed, coming out on top, winning a come-back attempt after nearly losing out to the garbage heap.

Artist Stephen Whittlesey, based in Barnstable, Massachusetts, makes sculptural furniture from architectural details and scrap wood salvaged from building sites. The pieces display the effects of time, the shadows of what used to be—nail holes, layers of paint, marks of vanished hardware. Whittlesey's salvaged pieces incorporate complex, layered components, each with its own mystery. Combined colors, textures, patterns, and forms evoke memories of the past; they resonate with implied meanings. In a world so

A wooden frame platform bed, covered with a worn but wonderful quilt, left, is supported on four bowling balls—an inventive solution to the problem of getting the bed off the floor.

One of Jon Bok's pieces is adorned with license plates, coffee cans, and the tops of tin cans, all flattened to create a seamless surface, right.

full of the slick and the new, older objects—enriched by time and history—become more and more valuable. Whittlesey's work inspires conflicting responses: on the one hand, his unconventional juxtaposition of elements is startling; on the other, the familiar motifs (staircase, cupboard doors, chair legs) are friendly reminders of known elements. Whittlesey specializes in turning one thing into another—a staircase becomes a cupboard, a cabinet resembles a children's playhouse.

Linus Corragio, a sculptor whose studio is on the Lower East Side of New York, is another who works with construction leftovers—but metal is his medium of choice. He makes use of detritus from commercial building sites and also collects items from the streets and sidewalks of Manhattan. He has made chairs and table bases from many sources, including wrought-iron filigree, metal rebars (used to reinforce concrete), and surplus street signs.

Folk Furniture

Found furniture can also have less intellectual origins. For every object described here, there are probably many as yet un-thought of hovering in the minds of inspired furniture makers and folk artists. Folk furniture is often made by anonymous, humble artisans, generally elderly persons who take up a craft—chair making, for example—late in life, perhaps after they have retired from their regular jobs. Some folk furniture is made by marginal figures. Examples include a child's desk made by an ex-slave or a tramp-art chest made out of cigar-box wood with chip-carved decoration. Each bears the individual stamp of its creator, yet remains anonymous.

Folk furniture makers come to the craft in various ways. Leroy Person was an illiterate sawmill worker in North Carolina. He retired at the age of seventy, and soon after began making striking furniture using found furniture parts and scrap wood incised in linear patterns. Each piece was then slathered with a single color of paint. Everything he used—the wood, the furniture parts, even the paint—was leftover, found material.

Folk furniture can be made out of all different kinds of found materials, from twigs to horseshoes, which are a very popular material for this type of furniture. Sometimes the horseshoes are painted different colors; one example has horseshoes and metal pieces spelling out BABY across the back.

Rustic furniture, crafted from twigs and unpeeled tree branches, is a venerable tradition that makes a good fit with the folk method. Materials are "found" in the woods, then are bent, looped, and woven into charming, intricate furniture. Michigan-based Clifton Monteith is a reinterpreter of twig furniture. His pieces could be described as semiwild, somewhere between a tangled forest thicket and a wing chair. Daniel Mack, a custom furniture maker with a studio in New York City, also creates forest-inspired works. His come in two versions. One, with the bark left on, incorporates the natural surface of the wood, with all its scars, splits, and curves. The peeled style is dramatic and sculptural. He uses Shaker webbing for the woven seats, usually in a variety of colors.

Pop culture is another reliable source of furniture-making materials. A table can be made out of stacked beer cans, with a beer advertising tray as a top. Magic Markers make great decorating tools. Bottle caps, hubcaps, and flattened tin cans are terrific as applied ornament.

Furniture of Unusual Parts

Chairs

Chairs come in a number of different varieties. The chair is the perennially favorite project of designers and architects, who are always coming up with a new version, *the* version, or merely a topical interpretation. A chair can be nostalgic, aerodynamic, comforting, or arrestingly beautiful, but fiendishly impossible to actually sit on. A chair can be a work of art or a sculpture. An antique or merely secondhand chair can add a personal stamp to a room, the final touch that makes it yours.

A chair serves multiple functions. If you define it as something to sit on, nearly anything—from a sturdy cardboard carton to a rough granite boulder—can become a chair. If your tastes run to design history, chairs can provide an instant synopsis. Sarah Stallard, a furniture designer who lives in London, has filled her flat with a diverse collection of seating—around the kitchen table, in the living room, in the bedroom. She has everything from a pseudo-medieval Victorian armchair with a carved wood frame to the sleek chrome and leather chaise designed by pioneer Modern architect Le Corbusier. Her collection even includes a few miniatures. You might express yourself with an eclectic assortment of various dining chairs (why have a matched set when a variety pack is so much more fun?).

Chairs are relatively difficult to make from scratch, but they're easy enough to do over. How might an existing chair be altered? If it's an upholstered chair, it can be slipcovered or reupholstered (although this process can be expensive). The slipcover doesn't have to be a standard cover; it can have dressmaker details, such as pleats, tucks, or bows. It can be sequined, made of an antique textile, or even semitransparent (this works well to give wood chairs a new look, too).

If it's a wood-frame chair, there are myriad possibilities. The easiest thing to do is to paint or refinish it, either in a solid color or with freehand or stencilled designs. You can just paint portions, or do the whole thing.

The next step, which presents more exciting results, but is also more difficult and not so easy to undo, is to apply ornament. Here, your inspiration can range free. You can use anything from fabric to twigs to bottle caps. Of course, you must exercise some care; the applied materials will make the chair appear bulkier and may make it uncomfortable to

A tramp-art chair, sculptural yet usable, left, harmonizes well with a classically decorative mantelpiece, found at a salvage dealer's shop. Architect Brian Murphy used a surfboard for the back of this chair, right. It gets around on skateboard wheels.

sit on. A wood chair redone by an anonymous folk artist has twigs glued in geometric patterns over the entire surface. Another chair, this one of wicker, has carved and painted snakes inserted in the weave at various points. The effect is quite intriguing. New Haven, Connecticut–based craft artist Sally Prangley Rooney paints thrift-shop chairs and other furniture with wild patterns of her own inspiration—musical notes, coffee cups, cats and dogs—and adds cut-out design elements, such as sugar cubes and doggie bones, to dangle from rungs and slats, completing the picture.

If you know something about making furniture, you can try your hand at creating your own unusual chairs. Perhaps you're attracted by the notorious Surrealist chair made of mannequin legs, or Salvador Dali's sofa designed to resemble a set of pouting lips. Some designers like to use surplus industrial and machine parts to make chairs. A tractor seat is a good place to start. Bicycle handlebars make a fine backrest and arms and can be wrapped in foam for comfort. The finished product suggests Picasso's bull's-head sculpture, made of similar materials.

Tables

It's easy enough to make a table—if you have something that will work as a base, you just need to add a top. A sheet of glass or plywood often works just fine. Tables can be made of almost anything. At his New York City store, Lost City Arts, antiques dealer Jim Elkind has several examples of unusual tables, including one made of a giant clock face covered with glass and another glass-topped table supported by legs that are actually the slender nozzles of old-fashioned fire hoses. Other tables are supported on mannequin legs. One artistic couple made a coffee table out of a wheelbarrow. Artist Clark Robertson has made a table out of piles of lithographic stones used in making prints, topped by a sheet of glass ("Reconstruction," 1984, sold through the gallery Art et Industrie).

Brian Murphy, who likes to employ diverse and unexpected materials, has made coffee tables using stacked flower pots (alternating red and white) for legs, the ubiquitous glass top further supported by a wrought-iron grille. He's also made a table with a square of white picket fencing as the base, and another using a bale of hay.

Tile-topped tables are another possibility, perhaps made of leftovers from other projects. A side table might be made from piled boxes, then covered with a square of an exotic woven fabric and topped with glass. You can also glue a patterned piece of paper to a tabletop (try a map or an interesting poster) and then use several coats of varnish or polyurethane to make a tough surface (water-based solutions take less time to dry).

Table bases can be almost anything that will support the weight. After all, a traditional low-cost version of a desk or table can be made out of an unfinished door and sawhorses, or file cabinets; if you want something more stylish, let your imagination go.

A beautiful Beaux-Arts sink, used as a table, left, brings a strong decorative presence to this corner of a room.

Broken safety glass fills a hearth designed by Brian Murphy, above. Peeled tree trunks are topped with plate glass, cut to fit, to create occasional tables.

Soft Furnishings

Fabrics, wallpaper, and flooring materials also get in on the born-again game. These are not generally reused; instead, items offered for sale originate in troves of vintage materials that have lain undiscovered in attics, storerooms, and warehouses since the time of their manufacture. It's generally not a good idea to buy used fabrics or wallpaper and try to use them for any functional purpose; they won't wear well.

Secondhand Rose, an antiques store in New York's Soho, has a basement full of wallpapers from the forties, fifties, and sixties, as well as old linoleum, all in perfect condition. Owner Suzanne Lipschutz often has sufficient quantities of a single pattern to sell to people who want to decorate a room. Smaller amounts she sometimes uses herself as part of a wallpaper "collage" that decorates the walls of her various residences.

Linoleum can be used in a similar way. Sheets of vintage flooring can be cut up into square "tiles" and then laid in any pattern you like on a prepared surface, using adhesive. It sounds like a lot of work, and it is, but it does result in a unique floor. Leftover flooring tiles can also be laid in a patchwork pattern for a similar effect.

Vintage upholstery has its place as well. There are several people who make pillows out of found or antique textiles (look for them at flea markets or antiques shows). Some also re-cover upholstered furniture with antique material. They use all kinds of woven textiles, including vintage western blankets, old mattress ticking, or fifties barkcloth.

Judyth van Amringe heaps embroidered and fringed fabric to create luxurious, if unconventional, seating, right. The designer's love of unusual combinations inspired her to top the textiles with a "giftwrapped" handbag, found at a flea market.

Decorative invention takes many forms, opposite: A small lamp, made of beaten metal and an iridescent shade, shares a tabletop with a suave pique-assiette vase by Robert Bellamy.

Often, creative reupholsterers use combinations of fabrics and trim—perhaps an "Indian"-pattern blanket together with striped mattress ticking, topped off by a vintage velour fringe from the fifties. Ronnie Wells, owner of a shop called Manderley, near San Francisco, specializes in this. She also does pillows.

Patchwork quilts are another method of incorporating vintage textiles into an interior. You can use scraps that have personal meaning—pieces from clothing, curtains, sheets, and so forth, that evoke happy or sentimental memories.

Lamps

Lamps and lighting can draw in a diverse collection of materials. These might be thought of as distant descendants of Chianti bottles made into lamps—the wildest, most imaginative offspring. Virginia Rustemeyer is an artist who makes one-of-a-kind lamps from found objects. She likes them to have "some social significance." Her current group of pieces are from household appliances, objects traditionally found in kitchens. They include a rather Japanese-y lamp made from a blender, and another adapted from a mixer (the bulb takes the place of the beaters), among others. They are recognizable as what they used to be, yet are definitely no longer that; they're clever sculptures, not just appliances.

Industrial Finds

Even the most obsolete, seemingly irredeemable detritus of our society can be rescued and brought back to life with the help of a dedicated and innovative restorer.

Bernard Sampson, a sculptor who lives in Houston, is a collector of old television sets from the thirties, forties, fifties, and sixties. He rebuilds them, restores them, and tries to get them to work. Some he keeps for his own vintage TV collection (he has about two hundred), others he sells to his fellow aficionados. If the sets can't be salvaged, he builds his robot sculptures from discarded parts.

OvenArts, a small company based in Los Angeles, converts old kitchen ranges from the forties and fifties into functional works of art. The owner of the company, Matthew Fassberg, repairs and restores these old appliances. Then, to bring them thoroughly up to date, he re-enamels them with a durable porcelain finish in bright, contemporary colors. His stoves are black and white, blue and turquoise, red and yellow—he even provides control knobs in different or contrasting colors. He also does custom jobs.

Even car parts and sections of old cars come into it, as does surplus surgical gear. Andre Debreuil, a furniture designer in London, has made a stand from an operating-room lamp and a clock from car parts. Long Island–based sculptor Marc Miller has turned his love for cars and his interest in functional art to the creation of furniture from vintage automobile seats. One version turns the tail fins of a '59 Cadillac into a love seat; a club chair was once a Ford Cougar. In both cases, the taillights still work and can be illuminated as "mood lighting."

Simple, utilitarian things have a beauty all their own. These table and benches, left, are made of bare-basic building materials—a granite slab, two-by-four lumber, and concrete blocks.

Sculptor Marc Miller satisfies his pop imagination and automotive yearnings with furniture pieces made from sections of classic American cars, right.

Architectural
Finds

Searching for treasure in the trash? Architectural salvage may be the answer. Buildings are being torn down all the time, and much in the way of beautiful ornament and expensive materials ends up in the dump. Salvage is unique—in material or workmanship, or perhaps, only in that they don't make them like that anymore.

Some like to use salvaged items as they are, with chipped paint and weathered edges. Others prefer salvage that looks almost new. There's room for different tastes. The Victorians, for example, built detailed houses that remain astonishingly solid today. Some of these houses have proved almost impossible to demolish. Most prewar homes share a similar solidity and attention to detail.

After World War II, a growing population meant that more houses had to be built in a hurry. Higher construction costs and postwar materials shortages meant that structures just weren't built that way anymore. Another source of beautiful ornament—corporate architecture—suffered as well. Prevailing Modern architectural styles bent toward less decoration, and changing financial times meant that corporations were less inclined to spend a good deal of money on decoration for the corporate headquarters. In fact, nowadays, many of them use salvaged or recycled ornament to adorn their headquarters.

Architectural salvage is decorative and distinctive, useful for restoring old houses and adding character to new ones. Restoration purists believe that fragments and full fixtures of old rooms and buildings slated for demolition should be used only to restore old buildings. Others have a more flexible outlook, believing you can use it as works of art.

Of course this attitude is to be deplored when it results in the stripping of older buildings solely for their architectural and ornamental content. But legitimate salvage dealers can be a great source for bits and pieces of ornament. Even if we can't preserve the past as a whole, at least we can capture it bit by bit.

To make the quest even more interesting, try to learn as much about your bit of ornament as possible. Don't just take the dealer's word for it. There are reference books about architectural history; find out your favorite period and type. Perhaps you like Venetian Gothic or Queen Anne; perhaps company logos incorporated into a frieze tickle your fancy.

Where do you find architectural salvage? A number of places: general salvage yards, garage sales, flea markets, the town dump. In rural areas, try estate sales, transient auctions, radio buy-and-swap sales, or classified ads in local newspapers. Some professional auction houses and a growing number of retail outlets specialize in decorative and architectural salvage. The search requires patience and a discerning eye. Although that junk heap might conceal a prize, the rest of it is still junk.

In general, salvage outlets have higher prices, but choices are wide and often quite good. Venture into one of these emporiums and you'll find thousands of old doors and windows, molding and banisters, pedestal sinks, claw-foot tubs, lighting fixtures, and stained glass. In the end, your budget and tolerance for hunting conditions will determine the lengths you will go to find things.

Low-key architectural fragments—a bust and a painted tablet—combine with Beaux-Arts drawings for an overall architectural theme in this study, above. The expressive face of a stone building ornament is the focal point of this still life, right.

Creative Reuse

Of course, salvage items can require a lot of work to get them into shape. On the other hand, many people enjoy these signs of wear and think they're beautiful. Some will want to reuse salvaged objects for their original purpose; others will display them as sculpture or use them as table bases or room screens. That's where the "creative" in creative reuse comes from.

Here are some of the items commonly found in salvage yards:

Exterior ornaments: terra cotta gargoyles, carved keystones, roof ornaments, iron window grilles, ornate blocks of stone, wrought-iron gates, corbel brackets, fire escapes, front stoops.

Interior details: mantels, fretwork, gas and electric light fixtures, tiles, windows and window frames, French doors, fluted columns and pilasters, bathroom and kitchen fixtures.

Here is how some of these salvaged objects might be reused:

Gargoyles (if you're lucky enough to find them) can be displayed as sculpture. Older ones are terra cotta or stone; more recent examples are cast metal.

Iron gates can be displayed hung on walls or from the ceiling.

Mantels aren't just for fireplaces. Depending on condition, they can be displayed as sculpture. Many people like to transform them into headboards, often with the addition of mirrors.

Corbels are fancy ornamental brackets, used on a building's exterior. They come in a range of sizes and materials, from carved pine to cast stone and are best used to display single pieces, or, in pairs, as shelf supports. A set of four makes legs for a low table.

Standing on a marble plinth, this tiny angel lends its serene presence to a diverse cluster of salvaged objects, right, which includes a stainless steel palmette that once adorned a roofline, a bird's nest, and a collection of iridescent beetles. Displayed on a top kitchen shelf, right, a fork-shaped finial in weathered metal juxtaposes dramatically with an old tractor seat and a collection of cobalt-blue glass, which in itself resembles a skyline.

Columns, depending on size, can be used as table legs or display pedestals (if you have one tall one, it can be cut down, especially if fluted). Tall columns (over five feet high) look grand on their own, lending a classical air to your living room.

Stained-glass windows can be displayed as is, used as room dividers, or hung in front of light sources, such as lamps or regular windows.

Shutters and doors can be used as screens when hinged together.

Molding and decorative trim (rosettes, plate rail, corner trim, wainscoting) add antique charm to a room.

Iron grates and grilles serve as tabletops (glass often added).

Fretwork (also known as "gingerbread"): fragments add decorative charm; larger sections can become room dividers.

How to Shop

The age-old tradition of do-it-yourself salvaging is alive and well for the brave. Demolition contractors aren't fond of letting you on the site, but you can always ask. They may also maintain salvage yards of their own. These can be good sources (along with scrap yards) for metal items. Places that keep items mainly for their material value will often sell individual items to those interested in aesthetic value (especially if you are willing to pay a bit more). Architectural salvage dealers are often specialists in certain items and

Inside a London salvage emporium, right, an array of milk-glass light shades occupies a tabletop amid other enticing pieces. Dealers like these provide a source for many fabulous finds.

often have higher prices. Some dealers place themselves in a semiantiques market, carrying upscale, high-quality goods and catering to a clientele looking for stand-alone architectural art objects. In this case, the items are usually known as "architectural antiques." Regular antiques stores often carry architectural items, especially as their popularity grows. Flea markets and yard sales might also offer some good buys.

How much should you spend? Supply and demand determine prices. Most salvage yards ticket items, but you can also try to bargain. The more desirable an item is, the more it will cost. Desirable items vary from region to region. High-demand items are usually very decorative objects, such as stained-glass panels or carved wood. If you do some shopping around and compare prices on similar items, you can get a sense of the going rate. Also, check prices and see what the item will cost new. In most cases, the salvaged item is about half the cost of a replacement and is usually of better quality.

The general rule, wherever you shop, is "Buyer Beware." Few salvage-yard operators offer refunds or exchanges. Check construction on wood items. Loose joints can be knocked apart and reglued, but split wood and broken joints are more difficult to repair. Cracks in cast-metal objects are almost impossible to fix. Missing working parts for mechanical objects can be hard to locate and replace. Missing ornamental parts can be lived with.

This is a strong argument against buying things that don't or won't ever work. It's difficult to find replacement parts for plumbing or lighting fixtures. So unless you intend to use something in a purely sculptural manner, make sure it works or can be repaired without too much trouble. If you're buying something to fit into a specific place in your home (such as doors, windows, or a mantel) make sure it's big enough (or not too big) to fit. If you plan to use old beams or columns structurally, make sure they're strong enough. Consult an architect to be sure.

The golden rule in salvage shopping is to make sure that the item is structurally sound. Otherwise, it's a piece of junk that moved from someone else's backyard to yours. While you will pay more for objects that have been restored, it may be worth it, in some cases. Most people, however, can take on easy restoration jobs such as refinishing wood or polishing metalwork.

Architectural Salvage in Depth

Aside from its decorative potential, architectural salvage has a practical side as well. If you're interested in using salvage items to restore or renovate a home, here are some of the things you'll need to know about buying and using (and when necessary, repairing) everything from stained-glass panels to staircases:

Stained glass is very popular and often high priced. It is often restored and used as an art object, hung in front of other windows or lit from the back. Check the condition of the lead channels that hold in individual pieces of glass (called *cames*) and soldered joints. Look for bowing or bulges in glass panels. Large pieces should have reinforcing rods. Stained glass salvaged from churches is often less expensive because overtly religious themes are less in demand. Detailing is usually done with vitreous painting techniques and may have faded somewhat. Be aware that inpainting (reapplication of color) restoration work can be quite expensive.

Window shutters are also very popular. Check for loose corner joints, broken slats, missing hinges, and rot at the top edges before buying.

High-quality, expensive carved stone is common at architectural-salvage houses. Ornamental pieces (terra cotta and cast stone, actually a composite material) are popular. Stone objects can be used as yard decorations or sculptural objects. Watch out for cracks and stains, as these are difficult to fix.

Don't limit your possibilities to old pieces only. These cast-plaster and resin replicas of architectural fragments, right, are available by mail order from Ballard Designs. Though entirely new, they have a convincingly weathered look.

Tiles are easy to find. Victorian-era encaustic or embossed floor and wall tiles, glazed ceramic kitchen and bathroom tiles are common. Old and new tiles can be combined. Crazed (cracked) finishes are not a defect. Some people prefer them. Avoid structural cracks—they are not worth fixing. Salvaged terra cotta roof tiles can sometimes be had. **Doors** are fairly plentiful in salvage yards. Be aware that the one you choose might have to be refinished. The trick is finding one in a style you like that is also the right size. If it's a new doorway, just frame out the opening to fit the door. But if the door is to fit in an existing opening, you may have to do a lot of searching. Make sure you know the exact measurements. An oversized door can be cut down to a certain extent (perhaps an inch either vertically or horizontally), but cutting down doors can weaken joints and throw off visual proportions. Pay attention to thickness as well—it's also an important dimension.

Look for corner joints that are still tight. You'll probably have to buy hardware; it's unlikely that original hardware will still be attached. You'll probably also have to buy the casing separately as well or have one made. The original hinges will have left their mark and new hinges will have to match in size and placement. Usually, though, you can switch the way the door is hung (left to right or right to left) without trouble. However, raised-panel doors often have panels on only one side, so make sure that panels will face the way you want.

Two ways to display salvaged Victorian stained glass, right and opposite, for an airy and open effect: installed in a bathroom window and in doors at either end of a skylit hallway.

Windows are hard to match to existing openings. A new sash (purchased from millworks) is often easier to use. Check for rot and loose joints. Make sure you match profile to existing windows if this is a concern. Old window glass is occasionally stocked in salvage yards. Old-time "wavy" crown and cylindrical glass is a high-demand item so expect to pay more. Most old window glass comes in standard sizes, but is difficult to install without breaking, so you'll have to allow for loss from breakage. Buy extra. Windows with elaborate designs (such as diamond or lattice panes) are often more expensive.

Molding and trim is usually sold by the foot, *panelling* by the square foot.

Cornice brackets and decorative door-plinth blocks are sold individually. Wood type, complexity of details, and condition often determine price. Paint can be stripped, minor damage repaired, but if it's really bashed up it's probably not worth buying.

Brick is more commonly found in demolition yards than in salvage houses as it is expensive to clean, transport, and repair. Unusual items such as paving bricks, items with raised designs, unusual colors or glazed finishes, may sometimes be found in architectural salvage yards, however. Due to the costs just mentioned, salvaged brick is often more expensive than new brick. Also, keep in mind that you can't use common bricks for patios, pathways, or chimneys. You must use hardened bricks that were intended for use as pavers or fire bricks. You will probably have to clean salvaged bricks yourself (cleaned bricks are more expensive). Old mortar can be carefully removed with hammer and chisel or muriatic acid.

A cast-resin column from Ballard Designs provides a base for a circular glass top, below. The architectural theme is carried through the pedimented mirror and classically proportioned drawing. Stone objects are common finds at salvage yards and can be used effectively as incidental sculpture in the home, right.

Lumber and flooring. Dimension lumber is uncommon in salvage yards—it's not usually considered worth salvaging. The same goes for ordinary flooring and exterior siding. Here are some related things you may find, however: hand-hewn beams or wide-board flooring made of unusual or rare wood species such as chestnut, southern yellow pine, and northern "pumpkin" pine. Salvaged stuff costs more than new lumber, so use it where its age and patina can be seen and appreciated.

Salvaged floorboards should be free of warping, with joints in good condition. Remember that the thickness is an important dimension, especially if the boards will be added to an existing floor.

Plumbing fixtures can be high-demand, expensive items, especially funky claw-foot tubs and pedestal sinks (which can be priced at over a thousand dollars apiece in some areas). About those tubs: since the feet are detachable, make sure the tub you want comes with all four. Also make sure the attaching channels for the feet (also known as clips) are unbroken and still firmly attached. In general, check on the original hardware, since it can be hard to replace. A wall-hung sink, for example, is not a good buy unless it comes with all its hanger hardware.

The working parts of old toilets are easy to replace (and usually will have been before you buy). Hardware such as faucets, shower heads, and drains should have all parts because they are expensive and difficult to replace. Porcelain items should be crack-free, although crazed or crackled finishes do not affect performance. Porcelain finishes are often slightly chipped, stained, or cracked; avoid those that are badly damaged.

Scrap metal, whether discovered in salvage dealers or on the street, has a sought-after decorative appeal. Above, a rusted metal hot water tank is reused as a console table. An amorphous piece of found metal, opposite, has a starkly sculptural charm. Such objects are displayed most effectively in an uncluttered atmosphere.

Lighting and other electrical items will all have to be rewired (this is not difficult). Old ceiling fans are usually a good buy, because of their generally solid construction. Items such as period switches and doorbells are available but reproductions are often a better choice.

If your dream chandelier is actually a gas fixture, it can be converted to electricity at a reasonable cost. If it is badly nicked or scratched, it can also be replated but this may cost more than the fixture itself.

Staircases are usually available only in pieces. Since they were designed for specific locations, it can be difficult to install one in place of another. But salvaged components are plentiful, including newel posts, balusters, handrails, decorative brackets and scrollwork, and the panelled wall units that closed off understair areas. If you're looking for porch balustrades, similar elements are also available. Check salvaged columns for insect damage and dry rot (especially at ends).

Antique oak ice chests, old-fashioned wringer washers, and the like can be converted to other uses or simply enjoyed for their sculptural presence. But there is a growing trend to restore vintage appliances to their original uses with modern innards. Some are simply

reconditioned, others have complete new insides. Refrigerators and gas stoves dating from the 1920s and 1930s can be found in salvage yards, as well as cast-iron wood stoves and cooking stoves from the nineteenth century. These often have beautifully ornamented surfaces.

Mantelpieces are easily salvaged and relatively easy to reinstall. Check dimensions, including outside height and width, and inner dimensions, to make sure they will fit. Many of them (especially those dating from the Victorian era) have elaborate overmantels.

Be careful if you intend to strip and refinish your mantel. Many old mantels that appear to be solid carved wood are actually made of a variety of materials. Some of the decorative detail may be made of cast plaster or gesso, which may be damaged by harsh strippers.

Door, window, cabinet, and other hardware is often in good supply and easy to find at salvage yards. Broken or cracked items are impossible to repair in most cases and are not a bargain. Hinge pins should be straight. Plated hardware should be priced lower than solid brass or bronze and is just as functional (although badly scratched pieces are not worth fixing).

Collections
as Decor

An accumulation of oddball china, picture frames, and handbags shares this breakfront, along with many other objects, including children's toys, to form a cheerful and appealing miscellany, above. Another approach to collecting is to select one theme. In this case, opposite, old kitchen utensils have a surprising powerful presence.

Why do people collect? Is it obsession, delight in objects, a little bit of both? Collecting is a passion for many. Some collections have been passed down through generations, and have ended up in museums. Others have persisted only briefly and the gathered objects have scattered to new homes.

Collecting seems to have gained in popularity and changed its meaning during the past decade. Today, people create collections of everything from Old Master paintings to cookie jars from the 1940s. Collecting today means the acquisition of anything—preferably something with a history—to enrich your home. It's no longer primarily about acquiring items of strictly monetary value, although that plays a role. People who collect do so mainly because they have desire, money, and time—very few use their collections as a hedge against inflation.

Collecting has become fashionable. Objects aren't acquired only by eccentric old ladies or lonesome bachelors; many artists, such as Andy Warhol and Robert Mapplethorpe, have put together collections of decorative objects, such as the aforementioned cookie jars in Warhol's case, and Venetian glass vases, among other objects, in Mapplethorpe's, which have later sold well at auction.

In the eighties, it sometimes seemed that everybody collected something, happily hot on the trail at auction house, flea market, swap meet, and tag sale, looking for the latest, most perfect, have-to-have addition to their collection. Here is a list of odd things people collect, from the marvelous to the mundane: Letter openers · Corkscrews · Pressed glass · Perfume atomizers · Soda bottles (Houston housepainter Victoria Herberta has 7,000) · Marbles · Beer cans · Parking meters · Matchbooks · Bicycles · Canes · Jigsaw puzzles · Buttons · Sheriffs' badges (Elvis Presley) · Cowboy boots.

Generally, collections seem to fall into one of three types. There's the theme collection—food, images of watermelons, Popeye, and so on. Then there's the object collection—toys, fans, TVs. The third type is the material collection—anything made of a particular material, such as ivory, jade, or plaster.

Many collectors use their collections as a source of decorating inspiration. For them, it seems, the whole process of gathering objects and materials that they feel are beautiful, rare, or of special value pales besides the thrill of arranging their collection for presentation. Designer and decorator Joseph Holtzman, for example, has residences in both New York and Baltimore. He makes use of several collections to decorate his apartments: miniature chairs, doll furniture, doll's heads, and lamp bases are some of the objects represented in his possession.

Others see their collections as a source of scholarly information. Alan Suddon, a retired Toronto librarian, often gives lectures about items in his collection of antique dresses and accessories. His son, Tom, seems to have inherited the collecting bug. He has amassed a large amount of British royal family memorabilia.

Still others seem to succumb to a less than academic seduction, collecting "fun" objects relating to pigs, cows, and toys, among other examples. Some collections don't even spring from a true collector's urge at all. Many people, not really intending to amass collections, have mentioned to a relative or friend that they like cats, say, and for birthdays and Christmas and any other possible occasion for years thereafter have received cat-related objects until, willy-nilly, they possess what can indisputably be described as a collection.

But this is not the kind of collection we're interested in here. To be a real collection, it is generally agreed, objects must be searched out, found, and acquired according to some overall plan, whether it is that you want to own all objects in the world made by a certain artisan or from a particular material.

Where to find things? Antiques shows, auctions, swap meets, flea markets, collecting societies, tag sales, your grandmother's attic (if you're lucky, maybe she'll give it to you for free). Cost: anywhere from fifty cents to several thousand dollars. Given these circumstances (the field is wide open), you begin to understand the excitement of collecting and why such a wide range of people get involved with it.

In recent years, prices of many objects have shot up: Bakelite jewelry, 1950s plastic purses and children's lunchboxes, Victorian fancywork, to name a few. What's the next hot thing? It's difficult to make predictions. Some popular collectibles of the immediate past were Biedermeier furniture, ceramics (chiefly Staffordshire pottery and French *faïence*, which is glazed terra cotta pottery), nineteenth-century children's tea sets, and souvenirs of all kinds. Objects of popular culture, such as souvenir statues of famous buildings and paint-by-number paintings (especially in their original boxes, unpainted), are showing increased popularity. Objects of nostalgic or whimsical appeal—mannequin heads, nineteenth-century games, vintage luggage—are another prospect, as are purely decorative objects, such as miniature boxes and ruby or cobalt glass. Toys and children's playthings are also highly valued. Collectors of the latter items display a passionate involvement in the field. These objects have the advantage of nostalgia—the memory of things from your own childhood. What qualifications does the collecting of childhood objects require? Only a love of history and a delight in anything small and meticulously detailed.

Decorating with Collections

Perhaps the most important thing a collection, when displayed, can do is add personality to your home. You don't need to be a serious collector with membership in a society and your own personal curator to do this. Just start buying some things you like—peculiar straw hats and baskets, interesting ceramics, old tools. After that, it gets easier. Interior designer Paul Leonard gives this advice: "Start with the biggest elements and do something personal with them. Add furnishings with strong lines, quirky details, patterns that appeal to you. Use what you have, but edit."

The big reward of collecting is that objects from different eras and cultures become the decorative focus for your own room. Living with collections means finding the best place for those things you enjoy each day. For example, you might display some of your favorites on hanging shelves—shelves you design and make yourself to harmonize with your collection. If you collect textiles, for example, you might want to show them off by hanging them from the walls or draping them over stair and balcony railings, or even over substantial pieces of furniture. Western blankets from Pendleton Mills and Beacon Mills

Collections held together by a theme, such as this group of strawberry-patterned crockery, right, reveal differing interpretations of a familiar shape or pattern. A collection of restroom signs from around the world, displayed alongside toy saxophones and cow-related objects, left, shows strong affection for elements of pop culture.

A contrast of styles some-times results in the best of both worlds. The solemn look of a formal, panelled desk is increased further by some serious-looking pigeonholes. But this high-minded, hard-working piece of furniture is topped by wonderful, quirky models of lighthouses, some adorned with ceramic bits and pieces in the pique as-siette manner, right.

(about 1900 to 1950) have colorful graphics and reversible "Indian" designs and have become very popular as collectibles. Others collect quilts, or samples of different types of ticking. But the field of collecting today is wide open—from baseball cards to Biedermeier—anything that is personal, offbeat and (last but not least) affordable.

Collections also serve a function when you begin to furnish a house. A collection can often be the starting point for color schemes and style. In the New York City loft of architect Walter Chatham and his wife, Mary Adams Chatham, the decor mixes a collection of antiques, found objects, and custom designs. Mary Adams Chatham says, "We haven't spent a lot of money. The impact comes from the juxtaposition of different elements, giving everything a heightened sense because each object is different from the one next to it." Mary likes to experiment with the placement of objects and unusual juxtaposition of objects of different eras and materials. In their bedroom, for example, there is an antique bed and chair next to a custom-made dressing table inlaid with harlequin-style diamonds in various shades of wood. Columns salvaged from a nineteenth-century house in Maryland contribute to the casual yet hip decor.

A collection of dolls and stuffed animals, enhanced by framed prints of idealized children, creates an appropriate, whimsical theme for a child's bedroom, below.

Another advocate of this style of decorating is interior designer David Salomon. He has rented a barn in Southampton since 1980. Each summer, he furnishes his rented space anew with secondhand furniture, fabric remnants, ethnic textiles, travel souvenirs, and wicker, modestly described as comprising "nothing of value." The combined textures and colors create a living collage. This approach, though strictly speaking not a formal collection, masses various objects and types in an intriguing display.

When displaying your collection, it's perfectly all right to mix valuable items with ordinary ones. Keep the focus on the object. You can group your collection in various ways: some of the simplest are by material, by object, or by massing similar things together. They can be arranged on shelves and tabletops or hung on walls. Lots of things grouped together lend richness. Glass adds sparkle, especially when it is set on windowsills and arranged with precision.

What makes a collection good? If it makes you happy, of course. Formal collections must meet formal rules, but if you're putting together a collection of objects that expresses your personality, then let your own satisfaction and pleasure be your guide. In the words of Anissa Helow, a London art consultant (she collects fishing-related items, such as antique fly-rods and reels), "Anticipate the fads, look for variations on what is currently popular. Don't be afraid of whimsy and eccentricity." Fashion designer Joan Vass advocates a hang-loose attitude: "The world abounds with wonderful stuff." Her Manhattan loft reflects this sentiment in its collections: shells (kept in a pie safe from New Mexico), ceramics, World's Fair souvenirs. A collector's room, once it takes shape, creates a personal collage.

How to Go About It

How do you get started as a collector? It helps if you know what you like. It's a question of educating your eye. Go ahead. Buy what you love, listen to your passion. Trust yourself. Personal passions result in personal collections. Buying old things requires getting used to a few quirks. You must learn to accept the ravages of age—old things do not look brand new, and that's part of their charm. Collector and antiques shop owner Leslie Allen advises caution: Move slowly, she says, do what you like, experiment. Possibilities are wide: Use pattern and lots of objects, or strip down to just a few.

Many collectors start small—literally. Leonard Lauder, president of Estée Lauder, the cosmetics firm, collects twentieth-century postcards. He has over a hundred thousand items, including cards designed by artists of the Vienna Secession. He employs a personal curator. Lauder started his collection as a child. Taken South on a family holiday, he would proceed purposefully along Collins Avenue in Miami Beach, collecting postcards of the newest art deco hotels. As he got older, he simply bought whatever caught his fancy.

You don't have to build special display cases to show off your treasured collections. Left, three knobby walking sticks lean casually on the wall next to a small table holding a few carefully arranged bird's nests. More fun for guests than watching slides of your vacation is examining this collection of hotel keys from all over the world— hung on brass hooks on the walls of a billiard room, right.

Other collectors maintain a similarly casual yet dedicated approach. Tommy Simpson and Missy Stevens live in a house they built themselves in Washington, Connecticut. They are both craftspeople. Their house is decorated with several collections, mainly of humble objects: teapots, small mittens, buttons.

Some people allow their collections to take over their lives. Guy Taplin supports himself as a decoy bird carver in a cottage on the Thames estuary southeast of London. His home (which he shares with his wife and daughter) is filled with the flotsam and jetsam he collects while out on the water, observing birds for his carvings. Bits and pieces (cases of cork floats, sea-tumbled glass and brick, bird skeletons, ship's figureheads) are stuck here and there, nailed to the walls, propped on shelves, rolled into corners. Gigantic round buoys take on new life as sculpture. Old shutters and old signs are used as decoration. The aesthetic extends to the new bits as well: Painted wood is distressed with sandpaper to soften it. Pieces of wood salvaged from old boats are a recurring motif. The prow of a rowboat becomes a hood molding above the front door. In this context, the large collection of bird decoys seems quite at home.

6

A Portfolio of
Lost & Found Design

In the Kroegers' living room, above, the beamed structure of the barn is painted a pristine white. The sculpture on the table, made of cut-down beams and seen in detail opposite, reveals the building's original color. The grouping of flattened and rusted beer cans by the hearth is one of Keith's favorites. The nearby sculpture is made of ice tongs and a giant drill bit and is affectionately named the Mother-in-Law.

Poetry Concrete

Susan and Keith Kroeger and their children live in a house full of wonderful found objects in Chappaqua, New York. The whole building, in fact, is a found object. It's an old barn, built in the 1870s, abandoned in the 1940s, then partially fixed up and lived in by a succession of people. Abandoned again after it had been used as a manufacturing facility for plastic toys, which went bankrupt, the barn was left to rot; the heat was eventually turned off and the pipes froze. Such was the state of things when Keith and Susan arrived to see it for the first time.

"The building was a real mess, all overgrown, when Susan and I bought it," reminisces Keith. It couldn't be further from a mess in its present state. Instead, it's marked by pristine spaces—painted white—that show off the barn's structure.

The Kroegers lead creative lives—he's an architect, she's a writer—and it shows. Keith's professional interests influenced his determination to let the barn dictate the course of the remodeling. "I wanted to make it a real minimalist interior. To remove it from time to some extent, so it doesn't look like an antique barn. To emphasize the space, the volumes and planes and geometry of the structure." He had respect for the barn's innate nature as a utilitarian, vernacular building.

"This whole building is made of very simple materials. It's all wood, a plywood floor, a beam—a barn. The whole idea was not to put in anything that was precious or an 'art' object. It was a conscious decision. Obviously, a few things have crept in, a few pictures. But for the most part, the things that are around are these so-called found objects."

In addition to those choices determined by the nature of the barn, Keith's and Susan's

own preferences are for everyday objects that also comment, sometimes subtly, on the nature of art. "I think that of all art forms, my favorite is collage," Keith says. "It's a uniquely modern art form, and of course it has a lot to do with found objects. And found objects intrigue me. Ever since the industrial revolution, we've had this tremendous proliferation of things in the world—things that have outlived their usefulness, items that were made to be functional, to perform a task. Curiously enough, many of them have an inherent attractiveness—gracefulness, even beauty—based on what their shape is, what they're made of.

"And much of it's also refuse, it's debris, it's litter. One of the most interesting things is to drive around or take a walk, and look down at the ground at the stuff that people throw away. You see very beautiful things. My favorites of all time are the huge trucks carrying the crushed automobiles. You know how they take them and crush them. And sometimes they still have paint on them. Abstractly speaking, that can be very beautiful. It's like those crushed cans—there's rust, and there's traces of color."

The Kroegers' interest in assemblage and collage reflects a major trend in twentieth-century art. Combined with Keith's architectural training and Susan's background in art history, this interest inevitably creates an emphasis on a formalist approach.

"Collage is assembling things," Keith explains. "This barn is an assemblage of things, a collage. An obvious example of this is the Pegasus—the Mobil horse that we've hung on the side of the building. It was made to advertise an oil company, to sell gasoline and petroleum products. It's a very beautiful piece of graphic design. Although Mobil still uses that logo, they use it on little disks. They've abandoned those great big porcelainized-steel, almost life-size horses. You see them sometimes sitting around old

A detail of the "jaunty" beer cans juxtaposed with the Mother-in-Law and a universal tool, right, illustrates the possibilities for designing with everyday objects.

gas stations out in the country. I found this one leaning against the back of a barn in Vermont. By bringing it back here and hanging it on the building, I'm creating a collage, using the building itself. That's how most of the things you see sitting around got here."

Keith brings the example even closer to home. "That thing at the end of the table is a stack of pieces of a beam that was taken out of this building when we renovated it. We cut it up and piled the pieces one on top of the other and made an assemblage of pieces of timber.

"It's called 'The Forbidden City,' because we went to see that wonderful movie *The Last Emperor*. It had great footage of the Forbidden City, the walls of which are that beautiful, faded-red color of stucco, which is almost exactly the color you see on barns. Of course, this is a formal piece, about structure, hence the name."

"Or 'Leftovers,' " interjects Susan. "We've called it 'Leftovers.' "

But Keith is not deterred by this frivolous note. He clearly has an enthusiastic appreciation for his collection of cherished and carefully chosen found objects. "I guess my all-time favorites, you can see by the fireplace, are those three crushed beer cans that are so jaunty, lively, and stylish."

Susan adds a personal comment. "He's a hard person to give presents to because he's so particular. But when we realized he liked crushed beer cans, everybody started giving them to him. Instead of two or three, we had eight or ten."

Keith adds, "Then from eight or ten, we had twenty of them! They were all lined up along that beam by the fireplace. I had to cut back to my favorite three.

"But that's very much collage," he points out. "It's a whole way of seeing things. Three-dimensional objects, round, perfect, and cylindrical, flattened into two dimensions, and they've acquired a nice patina of rust. It's a nice play on the whole idea—it's like a painting, an Andy Warhol painting of a Campbell's soup can, or a beer can, which he tries to make appear three-dimensional and these were the real thing and now they've been flattened into two dimensions. It's another way of seeing the same thing. It's amusing. It's typical of twentieth-century objects."

The crushed beer cans aren't the only found objects that grace the Kroegers' hearth. There are also some folk art–like things, among them an entertaining, if grotesque figure made of a giant drill bit and a pair of ice tongs, as well as a primitive tool and a cast-iron rooster. True to preferred form, each of these had a former life as a useful implement.

Keith calls the ice tong/drill bit assemblage a "junk sculpture." "We call it 'The Mother-in-Law.' It's a female form, a somewhat irate form. The rounded part in the middle is a boiler valve. The arms are ice tongs, and the top part is a handwrought hook."

The primitive wrenchlike object he describes as a multi-purpose tool. "I think it was probably used in conjunction with an old automobile. It has an amusing shape to it. A lot of animation." The rooster turns out to be more than merely decorative—it's a mill weight from the Midwest. "The windmills that were used to pump the water out of the ground had weights to balance the tails of the windmill, and they got in the habit of putting animal shapes," Keith explains. "You'll see these with cows and squirrels, and you name it. This happens to be a rooster, a very typical shape. It was a gift from a friend who collects them."

Away from the double-height living room, painted an austere white and chastely

banded by structural beams, is a bedroom wing. The low-ceilinged hallway is lined with cozy bookshelves. At the end of the hall, carefully spotlit, is one of Keith's most prized pieces, an old car door, displayed on the wall as a sculpture.

"The car door's a wonderful story," he reminisces. "I love automobiles, old cars and new ones. . . . They're very beautiful shapes, whether it's a hood, a fender, or a door. I'd had in the back of my mind that I wanted an old car door. One day, I went to the studio of an artist in Brooklyn whose work I like a lot, to buy a painting. We spent several hours looking at his things. I finally told him, 'There are two things in this studio of yours that I would love to have. One of them you can probably guess, but the other one you're never going to guess.'

"Over in one corner of his studio was a pile of junk. The car door was lying over there. We laughed, because I said I wanted to buy the painting, but I also wanted the car door. I loved it, because it has a great patina of rust on it, and it still has its little chrome handle. I think it's about a 'twenties Ford. It has a hole—a shotgun hole—through it. Of course, it makes me think of one of my favorite movies, *Bonnie and Clyde*, and the cars with bullet holes in the doors."

Keith pauses and becomes thoughtful. "So you see these found objects frequently have associations that go beyond just themselves. The door has a history. It comes from Maine, from a dump in a town up there. This painter picked it out of the dump."

"He was shocked when Keith wanted it," Susan says. "He was most surprised. He didn't know how to price it! He said he'd never had anyone want to buy it before."

Upstairs is Keith and Susan's bedroom with an adjoining study, tucked away in the former hayloft. The entire upstairs was roofed over when they found the house. "It was the world's largest attic," he says, still surprised that anyone could have been so blind to architectural possibility. The bedroom as it now exists is a charming aerie, full of intriguing objects. Chief among them is an old garbage can, worn, covered with faded turquoise paint, and wonderfully sculptural—another of Keith's favorites.

"When I found it, it was being used as a trash can at an antique dealer. I loved it when I saw it. I thought it was very beautiful. It's as though someone might have drawn it, but they couldn't draw the circle perfectly. The other thing is that Andy Warhol drew a similar garbage can. This was one of his icons. I think it's just as beautiful as the painting he did. It's a perfect example of a found object that has transcended function and become something wonderful to look at."

Keith says that he seldom goes out looking for a particular piece. "That's the interesting thing—we kind of let it happen. Here and there you just see things. That's the great fun about it." He has a special place for the first few objects that started his collection of found things. He keeps them in a library on the lower level of the house (the original barn was built into a hillside, so the bottom level is accessible from the front lawn).

"The first thing I ever bought is along the wall here. I think this was the first one," he continues, picking up a sculptural metal object that looks like an extraordinarily beautiful hook. "I'm not absolutely certain what it is. You can see it's nineteenth century, hand-forged. We think it was possibly part of a plow assembly. I saw this—back in the days when I started to pick this stuff up—and I paid a dollar for it. Part of the deal is that you don't pay a lot of money for these things. What I liked about it was that I didn't

Upstairs in the Kroegers' bedroom, left, stands their cherished garbage can, which reminds Keith of an Andy Warhol painting. An old washboard has a second life as a sculptural object. Another beam provides display space for a group of toy soldiers.

know what it was. But when you stand it in this particular position—and that's part of found objects, I think, how you position them, what you put them next to—it makes me think of some of the Calder shapes. It's very anthropomorphic."

Next to the hook stands another anonymous metal shape. It resembles an oversize, asymmetrical piece from a game of jacks, or perhaps something vaguely nautical.

"Most people don't know what this is," Keith says. "It's a nineteenth-century shoe-repair form. This piece, you see, is for a small-soled shoe, here's a bigger one, and this would be for repairing a heel. This thing can be stood up in any number of different ways and it takes on a life of its own depending on how you position it. It has a wonderful silhouette." Next to the shoe-repair form is another odd, tantalizingly familiar metal object. "This was a gift from a friend of mine, who brought it back from Australia. It dates from the era of the Australian gold rush. It's a hand-forged pick. This hole in the middle is where the wooden handle went through. These were the pointed ends." Like the rest of the trio, Keith appreciates the pick blade for its sculptural aspect. "It has a way of setting that gives it character."

In a small sitting room, right, the bare frame of a neoclassical chair is an amusing member of a conversation group with a contemporary upholstered armchair. A pale background highlights a few, carefully selected items—old cattle posters, flowers contained in a toy vehicle—in this basic bedroom, opposite.

In addition to this group of early-industrial found objects, the room contains some fragments of classical architectural ornament. Keith is equally enthusiastic about them, particularly a large cast-iron urn made in France in the nineteenth century.

"This has been painted and then sandblasted, so that you get a lot of the old cast iron, looking burnished. Look at the inside, it's all rusted. I think it's beautiful—the rust and the polish—I think it's a great combination."

In the end, it's that combination—of the naive and sophisticated, the raw and the cooked—that attracts the Kroegers to found objects. They are fascinated by objects that straddle the line between discards and sculpture, between art and life, just as their elegant home hovers between its origin as a rustic relic and its current role as a sleek shell accommodating a highly individual view of twentieth-century history.

Bottle caps, hubcaps, and southwestern folk art form a distinctly decorative hodge-podge in Jon Bok's house, above. No single item in this room is particularly valuable, yet the effect is that of opulence and richness.

Portrait of a Modern American Folk Artist

Jon Bok is something of a phenomenon. He lives in Los Angeles and makes "modern folk art" furniture and objects, carefully adorned with decorative bits of trash such as bottle caps, flattened tin cans, knobs, broken tile, and so on. A high school dropout, Bok had no formal art training other than helping his father, an antiques dealer, restore old pieces. Of the various jobs he has worked at—gas station attendant, gardener, mechanic, tire salesman, clothing store manager—none were art related.

He's originally from Fairfield, Connecticut. In the course of moving to Los Angeles during the early eighties, he got stuck in Tucson. His money gave out and he was forced to live on the streets for six months. During this period, he became familiar with religious iconography (churches provide free meals, he points out) and absorbed the Mexican culture that permeates the Southwest. He finally arrived in Hollywood courtesy of a bus ticket bought by a Franciscan monk. Now he's a successful artist. Many pop singers and movie stars own his pieces, and his gallery openings are always crowded with enthusiastic fans.

On the face of it, Bok makes simple furniture, with blocky, almost naive proportions. He transforms them with intricate surface decoration, using scraps of leftover wood to make chairs, chests, and lamps, covered with a collage of found materials—bottle caps, hubcaps, tin cans, dried macaroni, often a final touch of fabric fringe. Curlicues and cursive writing in paint and felt-tip marker cover surfaces otherwise unadorned. Side and back panels are inlaid with oil paintings found on the street, rescued from the garbage or bought at flea markets.

His work is overtly simple, without elaborate intellectual justification—he simply goes ahead and does it. The pieces have an eclectic exuberance. "Impure" materials—junk—are used to adorn functional objects—chairs, chests of drawers, crucifixes. "It's folk art," he says, "even though it doesn't look anything like that." Bok has a keen, offbeat sense of humor which reveals itself in a variety of ways. The drawers of his pieces are lined with Astroturf® or Mexican anatomy posters. A chair dedicated to Elvis Presley has "Returned to sender" scribbled on the back. The bright colors of Mexican art, labels from liquor bottles, and colorful Art Deco pottery are part of his palette.

He's also started to make some upholstered pieces. He especially wants to make comfy upholstered chairs, the kind your parents might have sat in to watch TV and perhaps have a nap. But the ones he's made so far, he says, are "not as comfy as store-bought stuff. I almost got it right—but you don't quite sink into it like a La-Z-Boy.

"My work has changed since I started. The decoration is more integrated. The earlier things looked more like furniture with things nailed onto it. A few years ago my pieces were funnier. Now they're more decorative."

Bok's philosophy of design and interior decoration is fairly simple. Hubcaps, antlers, Mexican folk art, rusted horseshoes, and papier-mâché skeletons are some of the things that adorn his living room. He also likes to have some of the pieces he makes around. "There are things I make that I wouldn't sell. Most of it I sell as soon as I make it so there are times when there's practically nothing of mine around in my house. I keep about two things a year so about every six months I get to make something and keep it. It's kind of a retrospective of what I've done."

What are some of his favorite things? He likes hubcaps. "By itself, a hubcap's a piece of junk. But when you get whole bunch together on the wall, they're all glittery." He's a knowledgeable collector, not just a scavenger. He can identify all his hubcaps and knows which kind of car they belong to, which year they were made, back to the fifties.

But he's not a car snob. Of all his hubcaps, he confesses to liking the smashed ones best—for purely formal reasons. "They're like pancakes, squashed flat, but you can still see all the details."

Bok has also come up with several ways of displaying his collection. One wall of the living room in his former house was hung with hubcaps. In the house before that, one of the exterior walls was covered with hubcaps, dramatically illuminated at night by colored spotlights.

He started collecting hubcaps when he lived in that house. It was in very bad condition. The exterior walls hadn't been painted in sixty years. At first he hung the hubcaps on the back of the house, in order to hide the peeling paint and to call the landlady's attention to the poor condition of the wall. But she liked the hubcaps so much that she was even less inclined to paint the house.

He's lived in a series of rented houses in Los Angeles that he's fixed up. He's gotten tired of fixing up and now wants to own his own home, although he finds Southern California real estate prices daunting. Still, it's clear that the process of restoring a nearly derelict house, of making something out of almost nothing, is one that he finds both liberating and deeply satisfying.

"I like junky houses. You can do whatever you want. My last house was a real mess before I moved in. It was a whorehouse, called the Ministry of Leather and Lace. There were all these junkies hanging around, no doors, broken windows. We fixed it up really nicely. We even did some landscaping. Then the landlord drove by one day and saw how nice it was and the next day he put it on the market. That's the trouble with renting."

He confesses that experiences like this have caused him to feel a little bitter about the whole process. He's lived in his current house, also a rental, for about a year and is just starting to fix it up.

He makes a distinction between the pieces he makes for sale and the pieces he has around the house. "I make my own furniture—I don't just apply stuff to existing objects. Well, except for my kitchen chairs, but that's just my house, my own home sensibility. For my own pieces, I build everything from the bottom up."

The kitchen chairs in question are Mexican rustic chairs (usually seen painted in floral designs), which he decorated with Magic Marker drawings. One has !!*%??#, *!!%#@ markings on the back slats, the kind you see substituting for bad language in cartoon speech balloons. Of these, he says, "I'm not into comic books really. I like the curse symbols—kind of humorous and grouchy at the same time."

Another chair is decorated with macaroni (the kind shaped like wheels and elbows), glued onto it in pinwheel and flower designs. The legs are adorned with bottle caps.

He uses lots of applied bottle caps and flattened tin cans, broken dishes, broken tile, weird wood—"everything I can find. I pretty much forage wherever I go. I'm always

Jon Bok is not afraid of juxtapositions others might dismiss as incongruous. A Day of the Dead skeleton on horseback peers from between two chests Bok designed and built, opposite. One is covered with can lids, detergent boxes, and bottle caps, with handles of bright glass mosaic tiles. The larger one incorporates license plates and horseshoes, as well as painted details.

looking for new stuff. I pick up trash and put it in the back of my pickup truck. I do well whenever people are tearing down houses. I find things like pieces of wood, lumber, broken tile. Lumber is really expensive otherwise."

In Los Angeles, he finds, everything that gets thrown out is relatively new. "On trash day you wouldn't believe what people throw out. I buy stuff in thrift shops too, especially the paintings I use in my furniture. I used to have a three-dollar limit on what I'd spend, but now it's ten dollars. The furniture is so labor-intensive, though, I can't spend too much on time and materials—or I'd price it out of the market."

He's got a gift for taking humble materials and using them in surprising, enlightening ways, so you see them anew. Despite his resolutely down-to-earth attitude, words like "miraculous" and "vision" are associated with his work, possibly because of his former eyesight problems.

Bok started building his folk furniture in the mid-eighties, when he underwent an episode of mysterious blindness. He had always wanted to make furniture. When he discovered he was losing his sight, he resolved to make one chair. The prospect of losing his eyesight made him feel that it was his opportunity to do all the things he had always wanted before it was too late. By accident, he discovered that making furniture was great occupational therapy. Building things didn't really require the ability to see and it kept him busy. "After all I couldn't do anything else I was used to—watch TV, drive."

It was the blindness that inspired him to use found objects as adornment for furniture. He couldn't drive to the hardware store, so he was forced to make do with what objects he could find walking around his neighborhood. "I've always liked junk. When I was blind, a few blocks were my entire world. I couldn't see much—I would walk into trees sometimes." But he could search out and find bottle caps, hubcaps, pieces of wood and broken tile and glass, and turn them to good use.

After his sight spontaneously returned, Bok continued to make furniture. "Then I had a party at my house. Someone who owned a gallery saw my pieces and offered me a show. Someone else there was writing an article about California furniture for *Connoisseur* magazine and put me in." It was that simple.

Bok keeps his distance from history and tradition. He's not worried about the distinctions between high and low culture, between pop and art. He respects only the limits set by imagination and vision.

He once described his influences as ranging from "Jesus to the junkyard." He says that used things simply have more personality. "Used as decoration, junk looks completely different." Ordinary items such as bottle caps take on a new aspect, appearing almost jewel-like. They convey an unexpected beauty of form as well as the cultural nostalgia suggested by the colors and labelling.

Underneath it all, Bok has a very sweet, straightforward nature. Talking to him, you get the feeling he just wants to be left alone and get on with it. "I don't try to offend people. I like my work to be humorous and pretty. Like the macaroni pieces—it reminded me of the projects you used to do in fourth grade, using macaroni as decoration, so I glued it onto some chairs I made. It's very sturdy, all coated in polyurethane—I haven't lost a macaroni yet. I make it so it's very solid. I don't want things to fall off or break. I live with it every day. It's folk art furniture but it's real furniture. I make it to last a lifetime."

A New Kitchen of Recycled Wood

Wood, especially when used in building, can lead several lives. It's kind of nice that wood is reused, going from living tree to use in an interior, to, perhaps, another interior, or recycled into furniture. Depending on the quality of the original wood, this can be a wonderful technique to employ. One of the best uses is as paneling, or as cabinetry. The rich, mellowed wood can be carved or remilled to create interesting details. Perhaps the best source is a salvage yard. The existing wood might originally have seen its first existence as floorboards or paneling. It's important that it not be too badly worn and relatively free from gouges and splinters (although it's amazing what can be sanded out).

Such is the case with this two-story mansion flat in North London. The flat's kitchen was designed and built by Igor Cicin-Sain, a Yugoslav architect who now works in London. The flat is owned by a professional couple who prefer that their identities remain anonymous. They are, however, willing to let it be known that they enjoy cooking, entertaining, and hanging out with their friends. What then, could be more appropriate than this cozy kitchen and dining alcove?

A cozy dining nook is framed in mellow wood, right. Curved shelf brackets echo other rounded surfaces in the room, left.

The warm tones of recycled wood dominate in this English kitchen, below and right. Constructed from a truckload of used floorboards discovered at a demolition site, it has many conveniences, including clever slide-out storage shelves.

The large flat is a typical maisonette, but the kitchen has a somewhat limited and awkward layout, a narrow L. To solve the existing problems, stemming from lack of light and inadequate working space, Cicin-Sain decided to turn the darkest and smallest part of the L shape into an eating area. While this emphasized the restricted nature of the space, it was also very cozy and formed an intimate setting for family dining and casual entertaining. The pale wood benches were custom-made and simple in style. This area of the kitchen is almost nautical in its attention to detail. Every inch is used, whether for storage or as work or eating space. Several clever niches, tucked in odd corners, hold necessities such as cookbooks, the telephone, and even footwear.

In contrast to the dining area, work surfaces are on either side of the window and thus get plenty of natural light. The counter under the window does double duty. It can be used to chop vegetables and prepare meals or as a breakfast bar for rushed weekday mornings or a more leisurely Sunday brunch buffet. The storage drawers beneath are accented with simple, handsome hardware. The walls and ceiling are heavily beamed, with white-painted recesses. The effect is of a barn, or perhaps a Tudor half-timbered facade turned inside out. The sink, just to the side of the window, offers a view over rooftops while one does the dishes. Above the sink, several tiers of wooden shelves, polished to a warm glow, hold a collection of sparkling glassware, coffee mugs, and custard cups. Above the door, another shelf, supported on curved brackets, accommodates a series of teapots in graduated sizes. Large-scale panelled brackets, similar in form, frame the opening to the dining area.

The biggest surprise of the attractive Old World kitchen is that it's not only new, but constructed from recycled materials. In order to achieve a properly mellowed atmosphere, Cicin-Sain purchased a truckload of old oak floorboards from a nearby demolition site. Judging by their thickness and width, they must date from the nineteenth century. These were partially remilled, sanded, and tinted with a diluted stain to continue the well-worn look (without too much evident disintegration and use). This served to amplify the innate elegance and luster of the wood.

The final touch was several coats of satin-finish varnish to enhance the wood's natural beauty and protect against further damage to the finish. Rounded edges and curved corners, wherever feasible, add to the cozy atmosphere. Some period bolection molding was also used to trim cabinet doors, along with handsome steel and wood handles. It's hard to believe that the final result springs from such mundane origins.

Necessity and Invention

Architectural designer Brian Murphy lives and practices in Los Angeles and has been crowned the prince of post-modern and post-industrial design. Everyday, ordinary materials learn new tricks at his hands. His chandeliers aren't crystal and gilt—they're made of barbecue grills or security gates. His utility lamps get around on skateboard wheels. Murphy's materials may be simple and inexpensive, but used out of context, they are striking.

Claiming to detest "high culture" and to prefer a "white trash" aesthetic, the Californian transforms humble materials with flair. Iridescent cellophane becomes a swag above a window. Astroturf® is used for carpeting. Vinyl sandbags pile up to become room dividers. He also likes to re-upholster flea-market furniture with such interesting yet incongruous materials as satin. He has a small but intense group of fans, including celebrity clients.

Murphy's wit has a Dada-esque, pop-art edge. Hula skirts, both kitsch icons and real elements of aboriginal culture, hang in doorways as curtains. He characterizes his designs approvingly as "Cheap, fast, and organic—the materials of the moment." He adheres to architectural theorist Buckminster Fuller's axiom, "Pollution is just an untapped resource."

Among his most popular pieces of furniture are chandeliers made from police flashlights suspended above a disk of shattered auto glass and wall sconces made of clear-plastic drafting triangles. These are the wild, imaginative offspring of Chianti bottles made into lamps.

Brian Murphy is the master of the apparently spontaneous interior, inventively bringing together an eclectic mixture of objects, furniture, and miscellaneous materials. For example, left, a vinyl "rug" is inset into the kitchen floorboards; an old advertising display of celluloid collars becomes a pop sculpture; and the furniture consists of thrift-shop specials wittily re-covered in satin and fake fur. A further instance of Murphy's inventiveness is a sconce made of a coat hanger draped with raffia, right.

Murphy grew up in Los Angeles, and once studied art and architecture at U.C.L.A. before dropping out. It's clear that he has an artist's eye, evidenced by his inspired use of discarded and unconventional materials. Before starting his design practice, Murphy spent several years working as a carpenter and contractor. He even worked on a house for Frank Gehry, the Los Angeles–based master of humble materials. Murphy doesn't mind low budgets and less-than-precious materials. He revels in the givens: what can't be changed. He's learned, through his experience on building sites, to exploit leftover construction materials—from tile to laminate—for his benefit (and theirs).

Murphy has invented his own language of materials. His past has left him with a taste for renovation—ripping down and tearing apart existing structures to create new ones. (He has built and renovated a series of houses for his own use, in each case acting as the contractor. These residences have served as the showcases for his theatrical and innovative style.)

Murphy's work devotes much attention to what's found on the site. He likes to make tacit comments on society and culture in the form of materials culled from the streets of Los Angeles. Architecturally, Los Angeles has almost no past, except for a few examples of Spanish Mission. All styles of architecture and design are possible here. Murphy's approach is a direct response to this—plenty of stuff washes up on the beach, whether it's real or just a metaphor. Nothing's permanent. In Beverly Hills houses are bought only to tear down; Murphy built himself a house and sold it nine months later. That's pure Hollywood style—temporal and much like a film set, built for a specific moment, transformed the next day into something else.

Murphy's design work echoes this dramatic, theatrical-set aesthetic. He likes to change houses. A house he designed for himself and later sold served as an exercise in

The dining room table was improvised from the slate top of a billiard table (the cutouts at the corners and along the sides were the pockets) supported on car jacks, left. In the kitchen, above, a diagonally placed island counter surfaced with a patchwork of high-style Italian laminate spoofs design trendiness.

interior design. Although it is deceptively simple on the outside, there are clues to what lies within. The driveway is surfaced in broken tile. The garage door is covered with palm fronds and china shards, but the brash details aren't all there is to it.

The house centers around an atrium containing a banana tree. The ceiling fan is made of bicycle gears, fishing rods, and silk. Everything in the house, even the oddest detail, has a practical use. It's a collection of great moments that also works as a whole. The visual play of layers, from palm fronds to crocheted hammocks, has a lively quality that is also highly ornamental. Most of the materials retain an insouciant California surfer sensibility. Windows are bordered with jungle prints; grass hula skirts serve a variety of purposes; a surfboard-backed chair sits on skateboard wheels. A neoprene wetsuit hangs on the wall like a sculpture. The whole interior exudes happy energy. Everything is straightforward but beautiful. The juxtapositions release energy instead of capturing it.

The very limited renovation budget let him stretch out and have fun furnishing the spaces. He makes it look easy. The seemingly randomly assembled settings get continuity from objects that keep contextual faith with the beachy surroundings. He uses typical Mediterranean materials—French doors, louvered shutters, tile, Venetian blinds, and lots of white paint—to ground the house and keep the interior cool and comfortable.

Murphy also reconciles handcrafted ethnic textiles and furniture with bits and pieces of high-tech materials. This mixture allows him to rebel against Hollywood glitz and retain the improvised, temporal quality.

One of his most photographed innovations was to use scrap pieces of high-style Italian laminate to cover the edges of cabinet drawers and doors in one kitchen, for a cheerful, multipatterned patchwork effect. Its quality of carefree innovation and absolute self-confidence allows it to succeed. The house displays other off-hand, inspired ways of capitalizing on unusual items: stacked raffia mats topped with glass make an end table; ordinary wire hangers from the dry cleaner's, draped with grass hula skirts, shield bare bulbs to create softly glowing wall fixtures; woven hammocks are suspended vertically and hung with more grass skirts, forming a room divider; peeled sections of tree trunks, topped with glass, serve as occasional tables throughout the interior; the dining room tabletop, originally part of a billiard table, is supported by four car jacks. According to Murphy, all of this was stimulated by a budget so low as to be practically nonexistent. In contrast to the improvised materials, however, is a carefully ordered background of clean white walls, sparkling glass, and colorful contemporary art.

Brian Murphy has been known to comment that while ninety-five percent of the people who see his work don't like it, the other five percent can't live without it—and they're clearly the five percent who count.

Left, more Murphy ingenuity consists of surfboards converted into furniture and used as sculpture, a coffee table constructed from picket-fence slats on an Astroturf® rug, and the final touch: neon-painted andirons. Raffia mats are stacked and topped with glass to make a casual end table, right. Genuine Hawaiian hula skirts form the room divider.

A Garden of Encountered Delight

Both down-home and sophisticated at once, a passionate combination of Texan enthusiasm and French flair, Robert Bellamy uses the time-honored European technique of *pique assiette* in a purely New World way. In pique assiette—literally, "stolen dish"—an artist uses ceramic shards to create mosaics, often applied onto the surface of a vessel, such as an urn or a bowl. Sometimes a piece of furniture is used as the base. In Robert Bellamy's case, not much is free of his highly personalized mosaic touch. His garden, in a suburban part of Dallas, is filled with examples of his freewheeling decorative approach, which uses found objects and trash materials almost exclusively. Bellamy, a landscape designer by profession, covers garden-store urns with bits of broken tile and china, as well as bits of Victorian glass and three-dimensional objects (such as doorknobs, a mannequin's finger, a light-switch plate). He also makes furniture covered with stuff—a game table with dominoes and dice, legs taken from an old stove. Through the juxtaposition of entire objects with representative bits of things—shards with symbolic power—Bellamy gives new life to fragments from the past; disposables (trash, really) are elevated to art. They become time capsules of the present and the past, snapshots of life's accoutrements, preserved in a positive way.

Bellamy, who studied art and has a BFA in printmaking, loves architecture and art history. In addition, he studied for a year in Europe. During his travels, he visited Barcelona and was deeply impressed by Antonio Gaudi's work, especially his unfinished masterwork, the cathedral of the Sagrada Familia (encrusted in mirror and glass, the Sagrada Familia is in many ways a forebear of all this stuff, a grand, high-art ancestor).

The exterior entrance wall of Robert Bellamy's house, right, incorporates random patterns of found materials—stone, brick, and tile. The doorway, left, showcases his offbeat mosaics.

Bellamy's garden is a collage of color, texture, and shape, integrating unexpected materials, a testimony to the power of New World wit and Old World know-how. He has incorporated debris from construction sites, bits of tiles, and broken crockery in mosaics. Underfoot are paths made of river rock, flagstone, and tile.

According to Bellamy, he's always loved broken-tile work, "the colors, the quality of little forgotten things preserved." He began by making small works, always using materials discarded by others. Sculpting with unusual materials opened the door to bigger things. But it was his encounter with Gaudi's work that provided inspiration. "I loved the Sagrada Familia, the different shapes, the dinosaur, the weird birds, the unfinished quality. It geared me up to go home and be creative."

The more he did, the more he wanted to do—and thus did his garden grow. He works on it between commissioned pieces and landscape jobs. "So far I've done around my front door, an obelisk in the garden, the front walk . . . I've worked my way around and in." The yard simply evolved, he explains—no formal plan exists.

While he is only able to work on the garden in his spare time, he is truly committed to completing it. He picks up material from building sites, from remodeling jobs that he's involved in as a landscape designer. He finds that people are only too happy to get rid of stuff when he offers to haul it off for free. He often uses pieces of tile from "keepsake" places, such as an art deco gas station in Dallas that was torn down. A section of his garden is paved with chunks of its bathroom tile.

Aside from the *in situ* work in his garden, he's been doing smaller pieces in an earlier tradition of pique assiette, also known as bits and pieces and memoryware, such as teapots, vases, and frames. He loves old garden statuary and cast-concrete pieces. These smaller pieces that he makes for others—vases, lamps, planters, some custom furniture pieces—have turned into a profitable sideline to his landscape design business. He has also created some "fun things" for local restaurants, using broken mirror along with tile. His furniture projects have included a game table for a private client with allusions to playing pieces.

"I love the older stuff—the texture, the roughed-out quality, the old-fashioned oozing quality—but my pieces are neater. I use grout instead of putty." He does have pique assiette pieces done by others as inspiration but doesn't have the space to be a collector, so most examples are things he's done himself and wants to keep around.

One of his chief pleasures lies in using things for other purposes: a drain grate is the centerpiece of his garden gate. The front wall of his house is a giant collage, full of pieces of torn-down buildings and trash materials, such as the very first Fiesta ware pottery he ever owned. When the pottery broke he saved the pieces and incorporated them into the wall mosaic, "because of the memories and because of the wonderful colors." While many of his materials are found, others are purchased. He sometimes buys imperfect tile at cut rates and then breaks it. More than half of his materials, he says, are trash. Other items, especially industrial debris and discarded building items such as radiator screens and drainage grilles, find a home in his work as well.

On the whole, Bellamy says, he prefers abstracts to works that tell a story, although his current piece is very narrative—a wall covered with a mosaic showing a "phantasmagoric" sun, with colorful clouds made of iridescent marbles. Beneath this he plans

A false "house" made of half-round logs forms part of the wall around the garden, reminiscent of a Western movie set, opposite.

Wire grids found at various construction sites around Dallas, as well as an iron bedstead, punctuate the straightforward lines of the weathered board fence, above. Croquet mallets stuck handle-down in the ground allude to a whole host of "proper" lawn activities. In a leafy corner, a giant pique-assiette urn—made from broken crockery and found ceramics—adds color and sculptural interest, opposite.

an entire cityscape, including skyscrapers with mirrored windows. A friend who's a metal worker is making him a humanoid figure of sheet metal which he will insert into the design, drifting out of the window. "I'm going to call the whole scene 'Urban Flight.' It shows how the human spirit is escaping from the city into the natural world, the world of my garden. It's a little touch of whimsy."

Bellamy's frequent references to the Garden of Eden are not inappropriate, for in many ways he has created a private paradise. His garden measures 100 by 70 feet and holds most of his found-object and pique assiette work, including a path made of meandering flagstones (the interstices are filled with a "river" of broken tile). Another path is made of black river rock, set on end in the European style. He describes his property as "a small house with a big garden with two fountains, and a real flow from inside to out."

The house itself was originally something of a relic, consisting of a garage with an apartment above. The house in front had burned down before he bought the property. In its earliest form, the house had five rooms on top, and a garage and store room below. Now there's a loft area upstairs with free-flowing space, and an office and kitchen downstairs. Like his garden, the house is full of surprises. The front door is set in a crazy-quilt freestone wall. Brick (from a demolition site, of course) forms an "architectural" frame around the door, creating an arch and scroll brackets. The tympanum of the arch is filled in with a broken-tile mosaic, as are the scrolls. The pique assiette mural above the door depicts clipper ships (existing bas-relief ceramic ships—whole tiles) in a "sea" of broken tile in blue tones. The front walk is made of flagstones framed in broken tile set between the edges of the larger stones. The large dark slabs are surrounded by bright bits of color. Mosaic-covered urns hold large plants around the door.

Outside the house, a concrete block wall painted white forms one side-wall support of the front steps. This wall (actually part of the front wall of the house itself) incorporates windows, placed askew, and is topped with a mosaic of broken tile. The tile topping has a jagged edge and resembles nothing so much as a bright blanket, tossed carelessly over the top, or a dripping layer of icing, poured over the wall. The top of the wall was directly inspired by Gaudi's work, says Bellamy. Studded with shards of broken glass, it resembles the spine of a mythical animal, a dinosaur or dragon, carrying a dorsal array of broken glass "armor." The wall curves up to follow the line of steps, looking even more like a dinosaur's rounded, humped back. Often, Bellamy uses mosaic to indulge his sense of humor and nostalgia. The mosaic wall contains some partial dentures (given to him by his father, a dentist), pieces of ceramic pots he made in high school and college, an assortment he describes as "pieces of your history and other people's, combined with the surprise of the unexpected."

Bellamy likes to put disparate things together and give them a new purpose, sometimes a whimsical one, as in his mosaic wall. Other times his combinations result in serene, almost classical beauty. He used old grayed redwood slats from a water-cooler tower and combined them with radiator grilles—"rusty and wonderful"—to make a fence on one side of his garden. The rusted grilles, inset in a wall made of wood slats, create a handsome geometry. The wood is laid in parallel squares, which are then set at right angles to each other to create a geometric patchwork. The grilles complement this arrangement with their own grids. The radiator screens make unexpected, lacy "holes" in the wood fence. Some are simple mesh grids, others have thick bars pierced with holes. Sunlight penetrates to "dematerialize" the wall, an unexpectedly delicate effect.

Unusual juxtapositions are a strong suit in Bellamy's work. An enamel sink—a school drinking fountain, really—is surrounded by formal cut-stone work and surmounted by architectural fragments. It's an unusual juxtaposition, but it works, framed with ivy and a persimmon tree growing up next to it.

Other, smaller examples of Bellamy's pique assiette techniques are scattered around the yard. Mosaic-covered urns are used as accent pieces throughout the garden to create a play of color and texture. Planted areas are defined by raised beds, bounded by retaining walls of stone with the occasional insertion of a tile layer or other materials. This has a random look, like a layer cake full of nuts and raisins. Other effects are more deliberate, such as a tall urn covered with a broken-tile mosaic in red, white, and gray with black grout. Other elements include architectural fragments and bits of carved stone. A favorite decorative touch is wide shallow bowls adorned with pique assiette on the inside only, filled with water and placed randomly on the low retaining walls.

Bellamy describes one wildly creative touch as his "snake fountain." "A friend who is a welder took four-inch bore pipe used to drill for oil and made it into the snake fountain. It sprays water and looks like the snake that charmed Adam and Eve out of Eden." A baroque construction of found materials, it has eyes of old-fashioned glass transformers, and nails for teeth. "It's just my favorite of what I've done lately. Next to the fountain I'm making a bench with a top of broken tile," Bellamy says. "Supporting the top will be lengths of pipe which will curve to become arms and end in snake heads. I'm hooking these up to a butane tank so they can serve as torches at night. They'll look just like fire-spitting snakes!"

One of Bellamy's favorite approaches to design consists of dismantling existing structures and using the components in wildly different ways. A boundary fence made from a child's play fort exemplifies this method. A client who wanted the fort hauled away offered it to him. He turned the timbers into a house with columns, set on its own miniature bermed hill with a tiny tombstone out front (found in a church basement). The structure, which originally resembled a small log cabin with a thatched roof, now looks like a frontier-town set for a 1950s western. The house has a tower above a little front porch, complete with a window and door. The porch roof is held up by carved-wood classical columns given to him by a friend. The window is filled with a rusty ornamental grille (originally from a downtown building). The door recess is filled with more of the half-round logs that form the facade. Tools and chopped wood shelter under the overhang—just like a real rural porch.

Casual juxtapositions can make for striking tableaux, as with these urns filled with giant bamboo stalks, set atop an impromptu table, right.

Bellamy likes the movie set effect. "The back looks like the back of stage scenery—you can see how it was constructed—but the front is completely convincing. The columns were about four feet high and almost perfectly to scale—I just cut off the bottoms. It was a fun way to solve the problem of a long stretch of boring fence."

As one might expect, Bellamy often finds himself the host of garden parties. The garden, he says, enhances parties by virtue of its unexpected materials and juxtapositions. "The 'fort' is really a fence. Then there's the snake fountain and the garden area, which is really straightforward." He also finds that the garden is useful in getting the spirit of his more unusual work across to clients. As a result of a private tour, he's now doing another snake fountain for a client. Of course, he does lots of more standard landscaping as well. "But I think this garden has loosened up my clients to take in more ideas."

A London Wonderland

The London house of Ian Allen, puppeteer, is, in the English phrase, "over the top"—packed full of lots of stuff, including ornaments, memorabilia, and furniture. "I didn't create an astonishing house; I just put it together the way I wanted it to be," says Allen. His first jobs were as a display designer in various department stores and clothing boutiques; so perhaps putting things together has at last come naturally to him. Now the house primarily holds collections of vintage Victorian and Edwardian advertisements, novelty biscuit tins (cookie jars) from a range of periods, and puppet-related objects.

In decorating the house, Allen put priority on purchasing such knickknacks and collectibles because they're hard to find. Carpets and other mundane items, such as sofas and mattresses, "can be bought any time," he points out. As is often the case with houses that hold large collections, the first impression of the interior is one of complete clutter, but it's really all meticulously and completely organized by size and by age and type. Allen leaves gaps to fill in when he finds the right piece.

In the kitchen, an enormous pine dresser and a cupboard take up lots of room along two walls of the kitchen. They hold collections of china and Victorian items as well as kitchen necessities. A scrubbed pine table and set of chairs are in the window bay. Allen hasn't worried about combining the two eras.

The dining room continues the mixture of periods. Chairs are from Victorian shop fittings; they are of the type where the customer would sit while she placed her order. Dog food sacks were sewn together to make chair covers. A display cabinet holds a collection of nineteenth-century biscuit tins designed to look like ladies' handbags.

The china-headed babies in the bath that form a centerpiece were once the treasured possession of an antiques dealer who unfortunately also owned a bird that used to peck at them mercilessly every time it was let out of its cage. The babies ended up in Allen's possession when he promised them a good home. A patchwork cover on the bed was made from vintage fabric pieces by Elizabeth Roll, who now helps to make puppets for Allen's highly successful Playboard Puppet Theater. He found her, originally, selling patchwork pillows in a street market. He commissioned her to make the coverlet.

The house is from the 1890s and, luckily, retains its period details. In the living room there is a carved marble mantelpiece filled with Punch and Judy biscuit tins. Carrying out the puppet theme, there are Punch and Judy doorstops on either side of the fireplace. An elaborately carved wood chair was bought inexpensively at a street market. Next to it is a statuette of the famous RCA His Master's Voice dog, head cocked and listening to the horn of an old wind-up gramophone.

Down in the cellar, the puppets are on display all on their own, without embellishments. In Allen's hands, each takes on a uniquely vivid life. The walls are hung with old seaside posters and enamelled placards bearing the names of train stations. These recount the places he has performed with his puppets.

The overall impact the house has on a viewer is one of variety under firm control. The density of objects is fascinating. The house as a whole expresses Ian Allen's personality. It's a quirky abode, somewhat eccentric and sparkling with individuality and ingenuity.

Puppeteer Ian Allen's London dining room showcases a collection of advertising art, from the dog food sacks sewn into chair cushions to more conventional tins, boxes, and enameled steel plaques, opposite.

Living with Architectural Salvage

Sam Milliken, a caterer by trade, lives in a house in New York's Greenwich Village that is a treasure trove of architectural salvage. Decorative items in the house include fine examples of stained glass, some of which are inset in door frames, others simply hung in front of existing windows. Carved stone corbels and rondels, ornamented with fantastic and grotesque faces, are set into the walls. The faces are a running motif throughout the house, popping up where least expected—in a bathroom or high up in a corner of a hallway. Huge cast-stone shells are used as giant light fixtures. A Victorian Renaissance Revival fireplace and overmantel occupy the whole of one wall in an upstairs sitting room. Cast-iron urns and lions' heads are dispersed about the rooms.

The overall effect is of space: large, bare, accented with pieces of ornament, elegant in an austere way. The salvage pieces stand on their own and are effective against the bare surroundings. The spare interior gives them room to breathe and be appreciated for their intrinsic beauty.

The living quarters consist of a large room on the second floor (the ground floor has a garage and offices for his business) and some cozier rooms upstairs, including a sitting room and a bathroom. Downstairs, the huge room contains chandeliers, some of which Milliken has had for many years, and unusual architectural items, such as a cast-metal Pegasus he bought at auction and several lions' heads made of various materials. The lions form a collection of sculptural items found throughout the house. Columns are another motif in the large room. An elaborately carved bar was originally in a restaurant.

The house is filled with objects from various periods, including a magnificent milk-glass pendant lamp, art deco in inspiration, selected by the house's first owner. In one of the striking contrasts that define the interior's understated, innate style, the lamp hangs in the curve of a bare-bones cast-iron and concrete stairway. The upstairs landing, roofed by a large industrial skylight, displays more examples of offbeat architectural detail, including wonderful carved faces set into the walls. Another cast-iron urn, painted white, has a tree growing in it, which Milliken turns yearly to ensure its even growth. An upstairs bathroom has a carved stone head above one end of the tub instead of an ordinary spigot; water gushes out of the head's mouth through a pipe. A turn-of-the-century shower looks like a cage of pipes.

The house contains things Sam Milliken found there when he moved in, combined with his own objects and pieces he bought at auction, from antique stores, and from salvage dealers. He was inspired by the house, which a former owner, an artist, converted into a residence. It was originally a turn-of-the-century parking garage (c. 1905) which the artist had stripped to a white-painted brick shell. He then incorporated various architectural items in the walls. The "found" nature of the interior influenced what followed. Following the lead of the original owner, Milliken acquired more architectural pieces. In fact, as he puts it, he has a basement full of the stuff.

"I think more and more people are interested in details. For sure, more catalogs are including this stuff. There are a lot of catalogs that feature this type of furnishing in

There are a variety of ways to display architectural salvage, and it certainly doesn't have to be put to its original purpose. Left, miniature columns bracket a love seat. Surrounded by mirrors and framed Indian prints, the giant Baroque shell, made of cast stone, conceals a light source.

reproduction—heads, pedestals, wall brackets, lots of other things. Things for the garden. I like to use real things, though."

The ornamental details contrast with the spare lines of the original structure. Milliken understands the complex interplay that goes on between eras. "An old house like this was basically once a commercial loft-type building. It's old, but to many people it says modern because it's big and bare and has clean lines and long sight lines. I like to juxtapose traditional furnishings in a modern space. I like hanging chandeliers from concrete ceilings. There's a certain simplicity about these rooms. The theme is simplicity and complexity next to each other—modern and traditional juxtaposed."

He's learned where to put things by doing. "You have to know what to do with these details. When you buy something you have to put it in the right place. It takes some imagination to fit pieces into an environment without making that environment look hokey. When you assemble a room you have to seek a certain harmony with what you've got. You try to find a way to put things up so it looks just perfect."

He's begun to think of himself as a collector. "I've had to look at each piece and decide—should it be on the wall, should it be freestanding, should I put it in the garden. Sometimes I think about the possibility of arranging some of these things like a museum. I want to put some signs up and have little cards saying where pieces are from."

Patinated metal lions' heads, once on the facade of a school in New York's Chinatown, now fill the spaces between windows, below. The Victorian stained glass was once part of memorial windows in a church. The Milliken residence is full of surprising contrasts—such as the classical rondel, carved with a woman's face, and the hanging lamp from the art deco period, right.

He appreciates that he is a custodian of history. "Maybe I should get a camera and photograph each one and write down what I know about it. To have a collection gives you a direction and allows you to communicate it to friends, the people that you want to share it with."

Although he has not been formally tutored in the mysteries of interior design, Milliken didn't work with an interior designer in creating his present milieu. He didn't think it was necessary and admits to having had a lot of fun buying things and arranging them just so. "I think that I'm happy with a lot and not happy with some of it. I don't think it's easy to come up with the right ideas. Maybe the easiest way to do it is to pay an interior designer a lot of money and even then you might get something that you don't like. Most of the things in this room were bought at auctions. And you get good value at auctions; you can get something that looks real and strong and you're better off—it has a lot more character—than just going to Lord and Taylor or Bloomingdale's and getting a complete room full of furniture. You see something that you like, and buy it, and then struggle with it. I think that's part of the process of buying interesting details."

Two different types of items that Milliken has grappled with and found effective places for are stained-glass panels, and carved stone heads and lion's-head ornaments.

"Most of the stained glass comes from a matching set. They're memorial windows from a church but they're nice, they're not too gloomy. Those hanging in front of the windows are three pieces that weren't put up anywhere when I moved into the house. They were in the basement. I said to the former owners that I'd like to have these pieces. We wanted them because they match the ones installed upstairs. How else would we be able to match them?" Although Milliken has hung his pieces in front of existing windows, he thinks that there are better ways to display stained glass, such as framed with a light source behind or in a cutout in a partition wall. Of course, he acknowledges, the best way is to set the glass into the window frame, but not everyone can do that.

He speaks with obvious affection of the various lion's-head objects that punctuate the house. "The two copper lion's heads hung between the windows [in the main salon on the second floor] were bought from the former owners. They're originally from a school building on Mott Street [in New York's Chinatown]. I got the stone lions on the windowsill from the former owners. I made the sills to show them off. They were in bad shape, painted and chipped and everything. I painted them with a stone-type color, to try and give them some realness." A glazed terra cotta lion in the upstairs sitting room is from a store called Lost City Arts in New York's Soho neighborhood. It's a recent acquisition and he's not sure he's got it in the right place. "I've still got to put something around it. But it arrived really fast one day and I had to decide where in the house to put it—I did not have a preconceived notion of where it should go. At first, I thought that the lion was too far over. Then I realized I could frame the lion with prints—I've got a lot of Indian prints—and make a pattern around the lion and it would be great!"

Where does he find everything? "At auctions. I do enjoy getting things through auctions. Mainly in New York City—William Tepper, and the Doyle in Manhattan. I don't go to the big auction houses. I look at antiques shops, but I tend not to buy there because it's likely to cost three times as much as it would at auction."

In the end, Milliken feels that the architectural details in his home work well because they fit in with his outgoing personality and hospitable lifestyle. "I like parties—I like giving parties—and so I find that these have great appeal to me. For the original reason that they were made—for people to enjoy. These fragments are strong. They have a life of their own. They're mythic in nature, they're fantasy things."

A second shell, twin to the one in the sitting room, turns the bathroom into a whimsical, romantic grotto, opposite. A small carved face, set in the wall above the tub, adds to the atmosphere. Water flows from a pipe in the mouth of another bas-relief head embedded in the wall at the head of the tub.

Eclectic Collecting

Judyth van Amringe is a decorator, maker of pillows and lampshades, collector, and (perhaps most importantly in her mind) dog lover. Her apartment is in far west midtown Manhattan, by the Hudson River, in a huge converted manufacturing building near the garment district and the Javits Convention Center. It's a shabby, off-the-beaten-track area. Nothing on the outside of the building (not even the rather faded but grand trompe l'oeil mural) prepares you for what lies inside.

Two black Standard poodles, Bix and Ruby, greet you enthusiastically as you enter. The apartment is packed full of stuff, furnished with a mélange of singular items from the more eccentric reaches of art nouveau and Victoriana, as well as found objects of no particular provenance—"odd bits," as van Amringe calls them, as good a description as any. Her apartment reveals a sure eye for detail and a consistent sense of personal style. It's a deft combination of precious (tapestries, silver candleholders and vases, carved picture frames) and artless (dog statues, carved bears, stuffed animals). Nothing here is of incredibly high quality, but each object is distinctive and well placed, giving evidence of a wonderful eye for texture and detail. Apparently, she's achieved the impossible—she

Judyth van Amringe expresses her eclectic interests in this collection of objects, left, which includes a sophisticatedly rustic table carved to resemble branches, a child's playhouse from the 1940s, and a Victorian decoupage screen, of the type once popular in the nursery. An unexpected way to display costume jewelry, right: A squared-off lampshade of burgundy velvet sparkles with bijoux and bangles, a noticeable contrast to the neoclassical base.

lives in a High Victorian fantasy, almost a stage set, but the apartment is relaxed and comfortable. The living area consists of two spaces put together, connected by a spiral staircase. Downstairs is the kitchen, dining room, and workspace; upstairs, the living room and bedroom. The living room area is dramatic and high-ceilinged, with a vast skylight; it's a former elevator shaft.

Originally trained as an artist, van Amringe got her start as an accessories designer, creating and selling wearable one-of-a-kind items. This soon spread from clothing to the home. She started applying the same sensibility to pillows and lampshades. People took notice and asked her to make things for them. Combining a love of old objects with an inveterate attendance at flea markets, she soon found that she liked mixing vintage fabrics with new materials or trimmings. One particular sideline has been lampshades, where she often integrates new coverings with antique armatures. Recently she's begun copying the old armatures to create a range of idiosyncratic shades in a choice of coverings, some new, some vintage.

Van Amringe recently opened a store in Manhattan's Soho district, where she sells pillows, lampshades, lamps, and the odd pieces she picks up at flea markets. As an example of her wares, she points to a small book-shaped box. "Like this little book thing here. This is an odd bit. I love little boxes. Anyway, I'm just going to be feeling my way—you know, the Braille method."

Judyth van Amringe's store is not just another antiques store, but an expression of her unique sensibility. "I just hope that I can find a few things, like the lamps, that are more interesting." The lamps in question span a range of types. Some are simply beautiful lamps, others are decidedly offbeat and witty. Some could be called "theme lamps," such as a lamp with a shade made of pages taken from a nineteenth-century German book. The base is made of piled books. Attached reading glasses (with rhinestones) add to the whimsy. Other lamps are more sculptural, such as one with a high-gloss black-lacquered conical shade. A vase-shaped, vaguely neoclassical lamp base has a square magenta velvet shade covered with glittery rhinestone pins and earrings.

Aside from the humorous lamps and the wonderful textiles, the things that strike the eye in van Amringe's apartment are furniture and objects—often striking, seemingly one of a kind—and the consummate savvy with which they have been placed. Not everyone could achieve this triumph of personal style. Fashion, art, and interior design—all these disciplines have shaped her intuitions and decisions. It's partly, of course, just because she has a lot of determination and self-confidence. She claims this, along with serendipity, as the wellspring of her many creative endeavors.

"The whole fashion thing started that way, because I always made my own clothes. And not wanting to work for anybody ever again in my life. That was the problem with being a decorator—I couldn't make a decision. Well, I could make a decision but then I had to ask whether it was okay. I'm not used to that. Especially when you know that you're right."

She's also very open to new ideas encountered along the way. "When I first started out in the accessory business, someone asked me to do stuff with rhinestones, and leather, and that's how I really got started. When I first started I said I hated rhinestones. I don't hate rhinestones. I love them."

In van Amringe's pastiche-Victorian bedroom and sitting area, above, ropes of pearls adorn a serious lady carved in white marble. On the back wall hangs a collection of more than forty frames, some filled with photos or prints, others with tarnished mirrors.

At this point, she's become very sure of her tastes and finds that her different inclinations tend to work well together. Her strong likes reappear throughout the rooms she lives in. "I like things that glitter. I like mirrors, too. I have a lot of mirrors around— not to look at my face, but because they give a reflection and another dimension. Mirrors are wonderful, especially old ones, with the rubbed-off gilt." As one might guess, she also appreciates metallic items for their gleam. She's partial to mellow copper, although tarnished silvers show up often.

Soft, plushy textures are another of her preferences. "I love suede—I like soft things and texture. There's something about texture—cashmere, velvet, even cotton—natural fibers. Then I like to layer over them. That's why I like stuff, too, because you can layer it. You start by having the patina, and that's its own layer, and add to that. That's why I like this carpet so much. To begin with, this was a fragment of carpet and now it's very worn out. But I like it because you can see where they put the pieces together."

She likes pillows so much, she urges everyone to have them. Lots of them. It's easy, she says. "If you like having pillows, just start making them. Get lots of old ones and then get trimmings and stitch them up—it's easy. They're just squares. Just sew it up. You don't need velcro and zippers. Don't worry about that. Just make one first. I don't like them anyway, unless they're really ornamental."

Van Amringe admits to a special fondness for Victorian things, ascribing it to the eclecticism so characteristic of that era, saying, "It's such a mishmash of everything. . . . It works here because this whole place is like a fantasy world, it's like a stage set. All this Victorian stuff in a real Victorian place would be too much."

In addition to a love of Victoriana, she acknowledges an appreciation for unusual combinations, at every level from floor to tabletop. She displays a full-size bear rug, for example, atop a flowered Aubusson. She also cherishes well-ripened materials. "I like carpets best when they get to the stage where you can really see the pattern. I hate pile; pile is horrible."

None of the stuff in her apartment is particularly precious or of museum quality. Clearly, she's been able to create a rich look without spending an overwhelming amount of money. She pushes aside the idea of hiring a decorator. "Some decorators do the silliest stuff but people pay a fortune for it. . . . You want it, and it should be cheap, but they see that it's $350 somewhere else and you can't afford it. And some crazy things get really out of hand—like 'fifties plastic handbags and those 'forties cookie jars. But if you're a collector, if you're really wacko about collecting things, you'll pay anything."

In the end, she finds that her pillows and lampshades satisfy her creative needs and also help her make connections with the outside world, repaying her richly with social and critical feedback. "I went to art school and thought I'd be a painter, but I could never sit still and be in that solitude for too long. I like to be up and mixing with people and getting ego gratification. So if I'm making a lamp, it's a minuscule painting. I get the same gratification and then I can sell it."

Being a savvy woman, van Amringe likes to think that she's chosen a style with a future to it. "I think about these salvage places sometimes. I asked someone, do you think this is ever going to end? And they said no, everybody's always going to want this stuff."

This corner of the living room, opposite, is a melange of different eras and oddball items—"odd bits," as van Amringe calls them. Set on the seat of a Biedermeier chair is one of her own creations: a witty lampshade made of book pages and decorated with a pair of rhinestone-encrusted reading glasses, set on a base of stacked books.

Sources

Architectural Salvage and Antiques

Architectural Antiques Exchange
709-215 North Second Street
Philadelphia, PA 19123
(215) 922-3669

Architectural Emphasis Inc.
5701 Hollis Street
Emeryville, CA 94608
(415) 654-9520

The Architectural Salvage Co.
727 Anacapa Street
Santa Barbara, CA 93101
(805) 965-2446

Art Directions
6120 Delmar Boulevard
St. Louis, MO 63112
(314) 425-0142

Baltimore City Salvage Depot
213 West Pratte Street
Baltimore, MD 21201
(301) 369-4599

The Bank Antiques
1824 Felicity Street
New Orleans, LA 70015
(504) 523-6055

Gargoyles Limited
512 Third Street
Philadelphia, PA 19147
(215) 629-1700

The Great American Salvage Co.
3 Main Street
Montpelier, VT 05602
(802) 233-7711

34 Cooper Square
New York, NY 10003
(212) 505-0070

97 Crown Street
New Haven, CT 06508
(203) 624-1009

Route 50
Aldie, VA 22001
(703) 327-6159

1722 Hendrick Avenue
Jacksonville, FL 32207
(904) 396-8081

Irreplaceable Artifacts
14 Second Avenue
New York, NY 10003
(212) 777-2900

London Architectural Salvage Company
Mark Street off of Paul Street
London EC2 England
071 739 0448

Lost City Arts
275 Lafayette Street
New York, NY 10012
(212) 941-8025

Nostalgia Architectural Antiques
307 Stiles Avenue
Savannah, GA 31401
(912) 232-2324

Old Mansions Co.
1305 Blue Hill Avenue
Mattapan, MA 02126
(617) 296-0445

Omega Salvage
2407 San Pablo Avenue
Berkeley, CA 94705
(415) 843-7368

Pasternak's Emporium
2515 Morse Street
Houston, TX 77019
(713) 528-3808

Red Victorian Salvage
1665 Haight Street
San Francisco, CA 94117
(415) 864-1978

Salvage One
1524 South Sangamon Street
Chicago, IL 60608
(312) 725-8243

Structural Antiques
3006 North Classen Boulevard
Oklahoma City, OK 73106
(405) 528-7734

Sunrise Salvage
2210 San Pablo Avenue
Berkeley, CA 94702
(415) 845-4751

United House Wrecking Corp.
535 Hope Street
Stamford, CT 06906
(203) 343-5371

Urban Archaeology
285 Lafayette Street
New York, NY 10012
(212) 431-6969

Webster's Landing
475-81 Oswego Boulevard
Syracuse, NY 13202
(315) 425-0142

The Wrecking Bar of Atlanta
292 Moreland Avenue, NE
Atlanta, GA 30307
(404) 525-0468

Artists, Galleries, and Shops

America Hurrah!
766 Madison Avenue
New York, NY 10021
(212) 535-1930
Antique Americana.

American Primitive Gallery
596 Broadway
New York, NY 10012
(212) 966-1530
Urban and rural folk art.

Robert Bellamy
Rep-Tile
1918 North Prairie
Dallas, TX 75204
(214) 826-4612
Pique assiette objects for indoors and out.

Jon Bok
% **Sonrisa Folk and Contemporary**
8214 Melrose Avenue
Los Angeles, CA 90046
(213) 651-1090

% **Art Mecca**
3352 North Halstead
Chicago, IL 60657
(312) 935-3255
Furniture from found objects.

Peter Clark Antiques
75 Main Street
Cold Spring, NY 10516
(914) 265-4389
Folk art.

Conversion Designs
118 North Lombardy Street
Richmond, VA 23220
(804) 358-3499
Hand-painted furniture.

Linus Corragio
Space 2B Metal Furniture Concepts
(212) 866-9556
Metal furniture from found objects.

Herb Creecy
27 Market Street
Barnesville, GA 30204
(404) 358-1687
Sculpture from found objects.

Rebecca Cross
℅ **Addison Ripley Gallery**
9 Hiller Court
Washington, DC 20008
(202) 328-2332
Sculpture from found objects.

André Debreuil
A D Decorative Arts Ltd.
35 Beethoven Street
London W10 4LD
England
071 960 3304
Furniture from found objects; design from unusual materials.

Gallery of Functional Art
2429 Main Street
Santa Monica, CA 90405
(213) 450-2827
Linus Corragio's furniture.

Carl Hammer Gallery
200 West Superior Street
Chicago, IL 60610
(312) 266-8512
Art from found objects.

Kelter-Malcé
361 Bleecker Street
New York, NY 10014
(212) 989-6760
Folk and outsider art.

Kimcherova
290 Lafayette Street
New York, NY 10014
(212) 989-6760
Unusual objects, folk and outsider art.

Donald Lipski
℅ **Rhona Hoffman Gallery**
215 West Superior Street
Chicago, IL 60610
(312) 951-8828
Sculpture from found objects.

Manderley
1101 East Francisco Boulevard, Suite C
San Rafael, CA 94901
(415) 457-4606
Pillows and slipcovers from recycled fabrics.

Turner Martin
540 Emerson Street
Palo Alto, CA 94301
(415) 324-8700
Antiques and found objects.

Daniel Mack Rustic Furnishings
3280 Broadway
New York, NY 10027
(212) 926-3880
*Furniture from twigs and other found
objects.*

Marc Miller
Art Furniture
2990 Huntington Court
Wantagh, NY 11793
(516) 783-4079
Furniture from old cars.

Brian Murphy
BAM Construction/Design, Inc.
1422 Second Street
Santa Monica, CA 90401
(213) 393-3252
*Interior design and architecture with
found objects and unusual materials.*

Virginia Rustemeyer
4331 Dexter Street
Philadelphia, PA 19128
(215) 483-4293

Room Service
4354 Lovers Lane
Dallas, TX 75225
(214) 369-7666
*Antiques, collectibles, old fabrics, recycled
furniture.*

Sag Harbor Antiques
Main and Madison Streets
Sag Harbor, NY 11963
(516) 725-1732
Antiques and folk art.

Secondhand Rose
270 Lafayette Street
New York, NY 10012
(212) 431-7673
Antiques and collectibles.

Timeless Treasures
192 Lincoln Road
Phillipsburg, NJ 08865
(201) 454-5649
Collectibles, folk art, and unusual objects.

Judyth van Amringe
107 Greene Street, 2nd floor
New York, NY 10012
(212) 925-4749
*Lampshades made from hats and
collectibles.*

Stephen Whittlesey
1560 Main Street
West Barnstable, MA 02668
(508) 362-2230
*Furniture from wood found in
New England.*

Catalogues

Ballard Designs
1670 DeFoor Avenue, NW
Atlanta, GA 30318-7528
(404) 351-5099
Reproductions of architectural artifacts.

Lillian Vernon Corp.
510 South Fulton Avenue
Mount Vernon, NY 10550
(914) 699-4131
Reproductions of architectural artifacts.

Flea and Antique Markets

West

"America's Largest" Antique and Collectibles Sale
California State Fairgrounds
Sacramento, CA

Reno Convention Center
Virginia Avenue
Reno, NV
(503) 246-9996
Once each year—call for dates.

Antique Peddler's Fair Antique Show
Trail Creek Village
Ketchum-Sun Valley, ID
(208) 345-0755
July 4th and Labor Day weekends.

Bakersfield Swap-O-Rama
4501 Wible Road
Bakersfield, CA
(805) 831-9342
Every Saturday and Sunday.

Kam Super Swap Meet
98850 Moanalua Road
Honolulu, HI
(808) 487-1477
Daily.

Outdoor Antique and Collectible Market
Veterans Stadium
Lakewood Boulevard and Conant Street
Long Beach, CA
(213) 655-5703
Third Sunday of every month.

Rose Bowl Flea Market
Rose Bowl
Rosemont Avenue and Arroyo Boulevard
Pasadena, CA
(213) 588-4411
Second Sunday of every month.

Southwest

Fairgrounds Antique Market
1826 West McDowell Street
Phoenix, AZ
(602) 247-1004
Third weekend of every month.

First Monday Trade Days
Highway 19 and Kaufman Street
Canton, TX
(214) 567-6556
Begins the Friday before the first Monday of every month.

Trader Jack's Flea Market
2850 Cerrillos Road
Santa Fe, NM
(505) 455-7874
Every Friday, Saturday, and Sunday.

Midwest

Ann Arbor Antiques Market
Washtenaw Farm Council Grounds
Ann Arbor, MI
(313) 662-9453
Third Sunday of each month, April through October, and the second Sunday in November.

Aurora Farms Flea Market
549 South Chillicothe Road
Aurora, OH
(216) 562-2000
Every Wednesday and Sunday.

Barn and Field Flea Market
150th Street and Parrish Avenue
Cedar Lake, IN
(219) 696-7368
Every Saturday and Sunday.

Caravan Antiques Market
St. Joseph's County Fairgrounds
Centerville, MI
(312) 227-4464
Several times each year—call for dates.

Country Peddler Show
Drawbridge Inn and Convention Center
Fort Mitchell, KY
(616) 423-8367
*Once each year, usually in July—
call for dates.*

Franklin Antique Show and Flea Market
Franklin County Fairgrounds
Franklin, IN
(317) 535-5084
*Third Saturday and Sunday of each
month, September through May.*

Friendship Flea Market
State Highway 62
Friendship, IN
(606) 356-7114
Twice each year—call for dates.

Giant Flea Market
Expo Gardens
Peoria, IL
(217) 529-6939
*Fourth Sunday of every month
except July.*

Hump-T-Dump
9510 Old US 31 (Oceana Drive)
Montague, MI
(616) 894-8753
*Every day except Tuesday and Sunday,
May through September.*

Hutchinson Flea Market
Kansas State Fairgrounds
Hutchinson, KS
(316) 663-5626
*First Sunday of each month,
October through June.*

Kane County Flea Market
Kane County Fairgrounds
St. Charles, IL
(708) 377-2252
First Sunday of every month.

**Larry Nicholson's Collectors Paradise
Flea Market**
Keokuk County Fairgrounds
What Cheer, IA
(515) 634-2109
*First Sunday in May, August, and
October.*

Mt. Sterling October Court Days
Mt. Sterling, KY
(606) 498-3785
*Begins at 6:00 AM the Saturday before
the third Monday in October and runs
non-stop until midnight on Monday.*

Scott Antique Market
Ohio State Fairgrounds
Columbus, OH
(614) 569-4912
Eight times each year—call for dates.

Snow Springs Flea Market and Park
Route 5 and Route 7N
Snow Springs, AR
Daily, February through November.

**Springfield Antiques Show and
Flea Market**
Clark County Fairgrounds
Springfield, OH
(513) 325-0053
*Third weekend (Friday through Sunday)
of every month except July.*

Tri-State Antique Market
Route 50
Lawrenceburg, IN
(513) 353-2688
*First Sunday of each month, May through
November.*

Wichita Flea Market
Kansas Coliseum
85th Street and Interstate 135
Wichita, KS
(316) 663-5626
Open various weekends October through June—call for dates.

Northeast

Amherst Outdoor Antique Market
Route 122 South
Amherst, NH
(617) 461-0600
Every Sunday, mid-April through October.

The Annex Antiques Fair and Flea Market
Sixth Avenue and 26th Street
New York, NY
(718) 965-1076
Every Sunday.

Antique World and Flea Market
Main Street (Route 5)
Clarence, NY
(716) 759-8483
Every Sunday.

Bouckville Antique Pavillion
Route 20
Bouckville, NY
(315) 893-7912
Sundays, May through October.

Burlwood Antique Center
Route 3
Meredith, NH
(603) 279-6387
Daily, May through October.

Crystal Brook Antique Show
Route 20
Brimfield, MA
(413) 245-3436
Three times each year—call for dates.

Dutch Mill Outdoor Antiques, Crafts, and Flea Market
3633 Carman Road
Schenectady, NY
(518) 355-3420
Third Sunday of each month, April through October.

Farmington Antiques Weekend
Farmington Polo Grounds
Town Farm Road
Farmington, CT
(508) 839-9735
Twice each year—call for dates.

Lambertville Antique Flea Market
Route 29
Lambertville, NJ
(215) 752-4485 weekdays; (609) 397-0456 weekends
Every Wednesday, Saturday, and Sunday.

Red Wheel Flea Market
Route 1
Freeport, ME
(207) 865-6492
Saturdays, Sundays, and holidays, May through October.

Renninger's #2 Antique Market
Noble Street
Kutztown, PA
(717) 385-0104
Every Saturday plus three "Extravaganza" weekends each year—call for dates.

William Spencer's Antique Show
Creek Road
Rancocas Woods, NJ
(609) 235-1830
Second Sunday of each month, March through December.

Malfunction Junction
7721 Highway 90
Mobile, AL
(205) 653-5549
Daily.

Metrolina Fairgrounds Flea Market
7100 Statesville Road
Charlotte, NC
(704) 596-4645
*First and third full-weekend Saturday of
every month.*

Scott Antique Market
Atlanta Exposition Center
3650 Jonesboro Road SE
Atlanta, GA
(614) 569-4912
Second weekend of every month.

Southeast

Atlanta Flea Market and Antique Center
5360 Peachtree Industrial Boulevard
Chamblee, GA
(404) 458-0456
Every Friday, Saturday, and Sunday.

Georgia Antique Fair
Interstate 75 and Aviation Boulevard
Atlanta, GA
(404) 872-1913
*Begins the Friday before the second
Saturday of every month.*

**Jeff William's Everything Show and
Flea Market**
Governor's Building at Kemper Arena
1800 Genessee
Kansas City, MO
(816) 228-5811
One Sunday each month—call for dates.

Joplin Flea Market
Virginia Avenue
Joplin, MO
(417) 623-3743
Every Saturday and Sunday.

Services

Keith Kroeger Associates
255 King Street
Chappaqua, NY 10514
(914) 238-5391
Architect works with found objects.

Manhattan Mansions
Sam Milliken
New York, NY
(212) 627-8388
*Parties catered on premises among
collections of lion heads and stained glass.*

OvenArts
2273 Fox Hill Drive
Los Angeles, CA 90064
(213) 552-1725
*Replace worn porcelain on old stoves with
bright new colors.*

Bibliography

Ames, Kenneth L. *Beyond Necessity: Art in the Folk Tradition*. Winterthur, Del.: Winterthur Museum, 1977.

Baking in the Sun: Visionary Images from the South. Lafayette, La.: University Art Museum, University of Southwestern Louisiana, 1987.

Bishop, Robert. *American Folk Sculpture*. New York: E.P. Dutton, 1974.

Cardinal, Roger. *Outsider Art*. New York: Praeger Publishers, 1972.

Carraher, Ronald G. *Artists In Spite of Art*. New York: Van Nostrand Reinhold, 1970.

Fendelman, Helaine W. *Tramp Art: An Itinerant's Folk Art*. New York: E.P. Dutton, 1975.

Gottlieb, Robert and Frank Maresca. *A Certain Style: The Art of the Plastic Handbag*. New York: Knopf, 1988.

Hemphill, Herbert W. *Twentieth Century American Folk Art and Artists*. New York: E.P. Dutton, 1974.

Horwitz, Elinor Landor. *Contemporary American Folk Artists*. Philadelphia: Lippincott, 1975.

House of Collectibles. *The Official Directory to U.S. Flea Markets*. New York: House of Collectibles, 1988.

Jencks, Charles and Nathan Silver. *Adhocism: the Case for Improvisation*. Garden City, N.Y.: Doubleday, 1972.

Manfredi, John. *The Social Limits of Art*. Amherst, Mass.: The University of Massachusetts, 1982.

Museum of American Folk Art. *American Folk Art: Expressions of a New Spirit*. New York: Museum of American Folk Art, 1983.

Rasmusen, Henry and Art Grant. *Sculpture from Junk*. New York: Reinhold Publishing Co., 1967.

Ricco, Roger and Frank Maresca, *American Primitive: Discoveries in Folk Sculpture*. New York: Knopf, 1988.

Walker Art Center. *Naives and Visionaries*. New York: E.P. Dutton, 1974.

Photo Credits

courtesy of American Primitive Gallery
14

courtesy of Ballard Designs
63, 66, 67

Jon Bok
45, 137

John Bouchier/Elizabeth Whiting and Associates
115

Tony Cenicola
27

© Steve Gross and Sue Daley
23, 34, 36, 44, 48, 50, 60, 74, 78, 131

John Hall
22 top, 24, 25, 52, 58, 59, 61, 64, 65, 72, 82, 83, 84, 86,
88, 89, 116, 118, 119, 121, 122, 123, 125, 127, 128, 132,
133

Mark Hill
21, 134

Lucille Khornak for American Primitive Gallery
37 left, 130

Balthazar Korab
13, 16, 17

Tom Leighton/Elizabeth Whiting and Associates
62

© David Lubarsky
32, 33

© Maxwell MacKenzie for Addison Ripley Gallery
37 right

© 1988 Norman McGrath
19

Stuart Miller
55

© 1990 Ira Montgomery
53, 106, 107, 109, 110, 111, 113

Fredrik Nilsen
46, 93, 94

Fredrik Nilsen and Edmund Barr
22 bottom

Spike Powell/Elizabeth Whiting and Associates
77

Tim Street-Porter
31, 35, 40, 41, 43, 49, 51, 54, 68, 69, 76, 90–1, 100, 101,
102, 103, 104, 105

Tim Street-Porter/Elizabeth Whiting and Associates
79

Jerry Tubby/Elizabeth Whiting and Associates
96, 97, 98, 99

Walter Wick
15, 73, 75

Index

Page numbers in italic refer to illustrations